Personal Development in the Information and Library Profession

Third Edition

Sylvia P. Webb

and

Diana Grimwood-Jones

Europa Publications
Taylor & Francis Group plc

Third Edition

© Sylvia P. Webb and Diana Grimwood-Jones 2003

Published by Europa Publications Limited 2003
2 Park Square, Milton Park,
Abingdon, Oxon OX14 4RN
United Kingdom

(A member of the Taylor & Francis Group)

A catalogue record for this book is available from the British Library.

ISBN 0851424708

First Edition published 1986
Second Edition published 1991
Third Edition published 2003
Reprinted 2004

Contents

About the authors

Sylvia Webb, founding editor of Aslib's Know How series, is a well-known consultant, author and lecturer in the information management field. Her first book *Creating an information service*, now in its third edition, has sold in over 40 countries. She has also lectured in management and inter-personal skills; her interest in this field led to this book *Personal Development in the Information and Library Profession*, also now in its third edition. She has written several other books, all with a practical "how to do" approach. Her most recent research looked at the introduction of knowledge management in legal firms. She has served on a number of government advisory bodies; been regularly involved in professional education and training, and active within the library and information professional associations.

Diana Grimwood-Jones's professional career includes several years experience of academic libraries (where she specialised in the Middle East), and the British Library. She became a consultant in 1992. In that capacity she has worked with a wide range of information staff in the public, private and not-for-profit sectors in the UK and mainland Europe. She is an experienced Distance Learning Materials designer, and has lectured and published widely on professional topics.

Acknowledgements

The authors would like to thank the following organisations and individuals for their co-operation and contributions and for permission to reproduce material: University of Birmingham; Centre for Information Research at the University of Central England, especially Pete Dalton; Dorothy Faulkner, Richard Taylor and Lauren Bell of Dartington College of Arts; Kathy Roddy of Kathy Roddy Research and Consultancy; Tracy Nolan at the Association of Graduate Researchers; Capita Learning and Development (formerly Industrial Society Learning & Development); Brendan McDonagh and Sophie Helliwell of The Work Foundation; Elspeth Hyams of CILIP; Sheila Corrall of the University of Southampton; Ashridge Management College; BDO Stoy Hayward.

We are also particularly grateful to the following individuals for their willingness to share aspects of their careers and for presenting these as case studies: Monica Anderton, Bob Bater, Monica Blake, J.Eric Davies, Jean Etherton, Michael Everson, Melanie Goody, David Haynes, Michael Oberwarth, and Leonard Will.

Introduction

Personal development or self-development is a complex subject; different aspects of it are discussed in various behavioural science texts. The purpose of this book is to define personal development in the context of the information and library profession, whilst not losing sight of the need to view it in a wider organisational setting. Therefore references are made throughout to the detailed reading essential to a broader understanding of the subject. The importance of seeing the library and information service (LIS) as an integral part of the organisation is also emphasised, as is the increasingly broadening role of the librarian or information manager. The book also discusses what personal development can contribute to the respective performances of the individual, the information service and the organisation.

The book describes ways in which this can be carried out in several types of organisation, for staff at different levels, and by various means, both in-house and externally. Those in each type of organisation will select ways most relevant to its objectives. To illustrate this, examples are taken from libraries and information services operating in both the public and private sectors, highlighting the different organisational influences on personal development. The qualities and skills required to manage a library or information service are discussed as well as the methods by which these can be achieved. Consideration is also given to the valuable role of the professional associations, formal and informal groups, and providers of LIS and other types of continuing education and training.

Problems experienced, including those of self-employed information workers, are examined, and suggestions made for resolving such problems, thus identifying potential areas for personal development. These are based on real-life situations, making them particularly helpful as practical examples of what can be done and how to do it. Various checklists and exercises are also included, along with examples of training programmes.

The book aims to be equally useful to those who have been in the information profession for some time, as well as those just beginning their careers. The words 'library' and 'information service' should be regarded as being synonymous, as should 'librarian' and 'information manager'. However these are by no means the only titles used to describe today's information workers and the departments in which they work. The book is just as likely to be relevant to those employed in knowledge centres, research departments, learning resource centres, IT units and others.

We would like to thank those organisations and individuals who have allowed their experiences and comments to be quoted, as noted in the acknowledgements. In addition we would like to thank colleagues throughout the library and information profession who have so willingly co-operated whenever asked.

Sylvia P. Webb & Diana Grimwood-Jones

January 2003

Chapter 1

What is personal development?

In opening any conversation on personal development it has been noticeable that the initial response has usually been based on an assumption that the topic under discussion is training. Whilst this plays an important part, personal development is a broader process, concerned with motivation, attitudes and personal qualities, as well as job-related skills. To put it simply, it is a constant process in which the individual seeks to enhance his or her knowledge, abilities and skills, and/or develop new ones; a process of continuous self-building and realisation of his or her full potential. It takes place by linking abilities with preferences to achieve personal goals, and applies to all aspects of the individual's life. For the purposes of this book it is in the context of the work situation that personal development is considered, but development of a professional nature and the resultant job satisfaction is likely to have a positive effect on life outside the work situation.

Those involved in the provision and exploitation of information require certain basic personal qualities as well as professional or technical skills and qualifications. You need only take a detailed look at current job advertisements to get some idea of what is being sought by today's employer. 'Dynamic and forward thinking', 'ability to work well under pressure', 'strong interpersonal skills', 'enthusiastic self-starter', 'good communication and team working skills', 'well developed IT skills', 'ability to teach client groups', 'project management skills', 'sense of humour'. These are all quoted from recent job columns, and describe what is required when appointing library and information staff at all levels and in various types of organisation. It is by building on such qualities that further development takes place.

The acquisition of management and communication skills can be as valuable as subject knowledge or technical ability. An information service fulfils the same basic function in all organisations, that of effectively co-ordinating, organising and using information. However, the emphasis in each is likely to be different, and so is the range of tasks or roles seen to make up an information service. It is this variety which offers possible areas and opportunities for personal development.

Who initiates this development? It does not just happen. Even if an opportunity presents itself, seemingly by chance, its full potential has to be recognised. The appropriate development then has to be thought out and, most important, worked at. More often opportunities have to be sought as part of a personal plan, and as this is being discussed in the work context, the organisation and the information service must benefit with and through the individual's development. This will certainly have a multiplier effect on the level of job satisfaction. Not only will the individual feel personally satisfied with each achievement for its own sake, there is also likely to be recognition by others of the usefulness of the end product to the organisation.

The following example still provides a useful illustration of this as well as of the way in which training can be cascaded. Back in the 1970s the first commercial database which Sylvia Webb introduced into the library and information service at Ashridge Management College was Datastream, and the database producers provided some initial training for staff. At the same time it was realised that having a terminal located in the library, as well as in the teaching rooms, where its use was originally planned, opened up all sorts of possibilities in terms of online searching. The next step was for two of the information staff to receive comprehensive individual tuition at the University of London's Central Information Service. This was particularly well structured, as those under tuition were encouraged to go at their own pace, attending formal 'hands-on' sessions at whatever frequency they wished. It created breaks of a length suited to each individual requirement for testing and learning in between sessions, and participants were encouraged to bring any special problems, including 'live' enquiries which they had experienced, to the next session. The result of this in terms of development for those who attended the course was general job enhancement and specifically the acquisition of additional skills, as well as a more comprehensive information resource for the College. There was also spin-off in terms of job enrichment for the other members of the library staff, to whom the training was passed on; immediate benefits in the provision of information to both academic staff and those attending the College's management courses; and an enhanced image which the College could project in its publicity material. Even though that particular example took place a number of years ago, and obviously the technology has moved on, the approach, i.e. interpolating off-site training with daily work experiences, and the spin-off gained through passing on the training, still acts as a very useful model.

To return to the question of who might initiate the development. In the example just given, the idea was proposed by Webb, as College Librarian at that time, with the organisation actively supporting and encouraging such development. The situation could have been different. The organisation might not have given its support. Alternatively it could have put the idea to the individual who might not have been convinced that this sort of progress would be desirable. In all cases such development must be well thought out, viewed positively and be acceptable to both parties, if the outcome is to be satisfactory to all concerned.

Although serendipity can always play a part, systematic planning is essential if an individual is to achieve personal fulfilment in his or her career. This does not mean that there will be a 'once-and-for-all' plan which must be adhered to at all costs. Quite the contrary. Personal planning provides direction, sets out objectives, identifies potential areas of development. It should not confine the individual; it must be flexible in order to accommodate unexpected opportunities and newly discovered skills and abilities; and must be regularly reviewed.

If you have not already drawn up a plan for your own development, why not do so now? It is appropriate at any stage of a career, whether you have just started your first job, or have been working for a number of years. Use the exercises that follow, keeping points brief and numbering each - the literary life-philosophy can come later!

Exercise 1

First some scene-setting is necessary. Draw a line down the middle of an A4 sheet of paper or its screen-based equivalent. On the left-hand side, itemise the functions/roles/tasks in which you are involved and the regularity with which they occur. On the right-hand side, indicate your degree of liking for each, e.g. (a) ENJOY, (b) DON'T MIND, (c) DISLIKE.

Figure 1 lists some of the items which may make up your working day. There will be others which you will wish to add, or you may want to be more specific in your itemising. The frequency with which each individual carries out a particular task and the amount of time it takes will also vary, and therefore is likely to influence the degree of 'like' or 'dislike' shown in the response columns.

Exercise 2: Analyse your responses

Now consider together all those which fall under each heading, and seek a common factor, e.g. why do you enjoy all those in Group A? Do they require you to use particular skills or abilities in which you are confident?

Are those listed in each group of a people-related, administrative, or technical type? Conversely, why do you dislike those items listed in Group C? Do you find them difficult, requiring skills which you do not have, or, equally likely, can you carry them out competently, but find that you actually prefer to do other things? Make a note of why you dislike them; that will take you at least half-way towards identifying what action needs to be taken to improve the situation. For example, if you dislike checking and clearing invoices, is this because your supplier is not putting the information you require on them, or because your internal procedures need

Figure 1. Itemising your working day (Exercise 1).

Functions/ roles/ tasks	Frequency of occurrence	Response		
		A ENJOY	B DON'T MIND	C DISLIKE
1. Enquiry work (list different types)	Daily	✓		
2. Scanning newspapers/ journals	Daily	✓		
3. Dissemination of information (SDI)	Hourly		✓	
4. Staff supervision	Daily/Constant		✓	
5. Staff training	Twice a week		✓	
6. Meetings	Weekly		✓	
7. Planning procedures	Monthly	✓		
8. Selection of information resources	Ongoing	✓		
9. Ordering procedures	Daily		✓	
10. Invoice checking and clearing	Twice a week			✓
11. Dealing with correspondence	Daily		✓	
12. Filing	Daily			✓
13. Photocopying	Daily			✓
14. Word processing	Daily - but supervision only		✓	
15. Computer activities (itemise)	Daily		✓	
16. Writing and editorial work	Weekly	✓		
17. Accounts & budgets	Monthly			✓
18. Professional involvement outside the organisation	Monthly on average	✓		
19. Work in other functions within the organisation e.g. committees		✓		

streamlining? List all tasks which fall into each group and put down reasons in a way similar to that shown in Figure 2.

Figure 2. Analysing your responses (Exercise 2).

(Only one task is given here as an example, but all need to be included in your personal checklist.)

Tasks listed under Group A (ENJOY)	Reason
1. Enquiry work	I get satisfaction from: being able to help people/ using my professional skills/solving problems/ carrying out desk research / searching the internet /contributing to the firm's business development. I like the constant interaction with people from other departments. Enquiries give me: the opportunity to learn about new subjects/ to use a wide range of sources of information, both print and electronic/ contact with other librarians.

On the other hand if enquiry work had been listed under Group C (Dislike) it might have read as follows:

Tasks listed under Group C (DISLIKE)	Reason
1. Enquiry work	I am never quite clear what is required/I have difficulty with unfamiliar terms/I don't know where to look/I worry about using the online services, especially finding the right web sites on the Internet/I am all right if people come into the library, but I have problems with telephone enquiries/ I could enjoy enquiry work if only there was enough time.

The latter response identifies problems in the area of listening and questioning skills and suggests the need for some further explanation of technical matters pertinent to the organisation's activities, more detailed instruction on information sources of all kinds, especially those in electronic form, more 'hands-on' experience, an introduction to time management and possibly some job redistribution.

It is quite common for creative people to dislike administrative tasks. Even if they are competent in that area, they see the need to perform such tasks as taking time away from the use of their creative or innovative ability. As most jobs do require some degree of administrative or organisational input, one answer to such a problem is to set up administrative procedures which are efficient but minimal in terms of time consumption. A practical approach to this is given in *Creating an information service*, Webb (1996a) where it is suggested that, rather than viewing such procedures as necessary evils, they can be set up so that they become positive assets. Your response may also be influenced by the regularity with which such tasks occur and the proportion of your time that has to be spent on them.

Another consideration may be whether these areas are solely your responsibility, or part of a joint activity with another department or individual. Of course there are many other variables which influence your response to your job, for example, your reaction to the total environment in which you work, its location, and your journey to work, as well as the more personal aspects of status, recognition and reward. Further consideration will be given to job satisfaction later.

So far the exercises above should have helped to provide a simple statement about your work preferences and abilities at a certain stage in your career, and offered a starting point for decisions about the next steps to be taken. The next stage is to relate these preferences and abilities to your present situation, and ask some specific questions, such as those listed in Figure 3.

Figure 3. Typical questions relating to job satisfaction.

1. What is my overall reaction to my day-to-day work, i.e. positive or negative?

2. What do I enjoy most?

3. What do I enjoy least and why?

4. Do I like the other people in my department and if not, why not?

5. How do I perceive the department in relation to the rest of the organisation?

6. Is there evidence that others perceive it, or do not perceive it in the same way?

   e.g. has the Information Manager or Head of Library Services got equal status with other departmental heads, in terms of salaries and fringe benefits as well as involvement in decision-making and consultation?

7. What is my reaction to the organisation in terms of its objectives, its structure and its perceived management style?

The answers to these questions will make apparent the need for a change of direction, or for continued progress along the same path, and any requirement for additional skills or possibly the improvement or updating of existing ones. Perhaps a complete change of role or a new emphasis in your present job could take place within the same organisation; alternatively a move to a different environment may be called for.

It must be emphasised that what has just been offered is a very simplistic approach, but can be a helpful way of starting the development process. It clears the ground and provides a base of relevant considerations on which a longer-term plan can be built. Some years ago David Fifield (1984), in an article called *Planning career success*, underlined the need to match corporate character and policy with personal objectives, and that advice still stands.

A more detailed method is described in A *manager's guide to self-development*, Pedler, Burgoyne & Boydell (2001), which is designed as a self-teaching work-book for those in almost any management function. Numerous areas in which learning and self development can take place are listed, and the manager is asked to select those with which he or she is concerned. Although many heads of libraries and information centres have always had to manage resources, i.e. budget, staff, stock, services, it is only comparatively recently that the management role has been explicitly stated as being an essential requirement for the post-holder. However, the book just mentioned contains a very useful chapter on self-assessment and goal setting which lists eleven qualities essential to becoming an effective manager.

These certainly have strong relevance to the management of a library or information service and to the librarian's personal development. That list, considered in conjunction with the exercises already described, could provide a valuable pen-portrait of career planning needs. Such work-books are well worth reading when embarking on the road towards self-discovery and self-realisation, whatever the professional environment.

Those in the information profession particularly have found themselves floundering at times in a sea, or rather a bubbling cauldron, of rapid change. The cauldron would seem to be the more appropriate analogy. Not only have librarians and other information professionals found themselves bobbing about in the pot surrounded by various technological ingredients, but also by accountants, lawyers and others previously not regarded as 'information workers' *per se*. This latter aspect could certainly be seen by some as threatening. Although those 'others' may not have the wide range of skills required to carry out professional information work, suddenly they are all (seemingly) able to use computers and therefore access information sources, of which they were previously unaware and for which they relied on some other person. The view that "everything is on the Internet" and that if the information sought does not appear to be there, then it does not exist, is still prevalent. While such instant access does not provide them with all the other skills needed for cost-effective information work, it does bring into being certain common procedures and shared knowledge which can cross the different management functions of an organisation. Rather than seeing this as a threat and sitting back in fear of being overtaken by events, effective management of such shared knowledge or activity can bring about positive benefits, in terms of enhancing the information service and the jobs of those providing it. It can be used to promote greater awareness of the potential of information resources and information staff and skills. The introduction of knowledge management (KM) has demonstrated this in various organisations, as shown in research into the instigation of Know-How databases in legal firms, Webb (1996b), with further examples from other types of organisation in Webb (1998). KM as an area for personal development is discussed further in Chapter 6.

In recent years there has certainly been considerable questioning of the traditional, possibly somewhat narrowly defined, role of the members of a number of professions. As the analogy posed above suggests, it is not only information workers who are required to broaden or change their approach, as well as extend their range of skills, but also those in such fields as accountancy, law, banking and others. Such questioning of tradition is healthy. However, it must be carried out in the full awareness, not only of the possible need for change, but also of the importance of adequate preparation for such change. This is not to suggest that old skills are merely replaced by new ones, but rather that there should be a building on existing strengths. As illustrated by the examples at the beginning of this chapter, today's employer is seeking a range of personal attributes as well as professional qualifications and skills. If those are the qualities that employers are seeking, you certainly have at least one good reason to think about personal development!

So how does personal development come about in an information environment? What is involved? It requires planning, as has already been said. You must work at it, continuously. The individual must maintain a constant awareness of situations in which personal development may take place, but at the same time make objective judgements of the relevance of such development to the organisation concerned. It may involve informal learning through group membership and related meetings, discussions and visits; or formal training. The latter could take place in-house or externally, and involve training in professional, technical or administrative skills. There could be ongoing workplace assessment either designed as part of an internal organisational programme or to meet the requirements of national schemes leading to vocational qualifications e.g. the Scottish and National Vocational Qualifications S/NVQs in the UK. Both informal and formal methods of learning may require additional activity in the form of reading, written or computer-based exercises, questionnaire completion, graphic work, oral presentations, demonstration of competence in various tasks and 'hands-on' experience. Other learning will take place within the organisation itself and will relate to the wider aspects of the work environment, involving observation of the organisation's activities and its relationships with the community at large, as well as the varied working techniques used by members of the organisation. Such observation and subsequent research will establish what information requirements exist, the sort of information service needed, the role of the information staff and the opportunities for their future development.

References

Fifield, David M (1984)
Planning career success. *Business Graduate,* September, pp.8-12.

Pedler, Mike; Burgoyne, John; Boydell, Tom (2001)
A manager's guide to self-development. 4th edition. Maidenhead: McGraw-Hill (UK) Ltd

Webb, Sylvia P. (1996a)
Creating an information service. 3rd edition. London: Aslib.

Webb, Sylvia P. (1996b)
Know-How and information provision in legal firms: individual knowledge and experience as part of the corporate information resource. British Library Research & Innovation report 1. Berkhamsted: Sylvia P Webb

Webb, Sylvia P. (1998)
Knowledge management: linchpin of change. London: Aslib

Chapter 2

The organisation and the individual

Computers, domestic pets and cars, especially your first one, are often referred to affectionately by a personal name, indicating a special bond between the person and the machine or animal. Perhaps in the case of the car this goes back to the days when the driving power really was measured in terms of the number of horses! Such warm, friendly qualities are not usually attributed to organisations. Of course, there have been exceptions, e.g. the British Broadcasting Corporation (BBC) used to be referred to as 'Auntie', whilst the Bank of England was 'the Old Lady of Threadneedle Street', but who has recently heard of an affectionate name for any well-known organisation? (Dear Reader, let us not set up a correspondence on this!)

Types of organisation

In what sort of organisation do you work? Is it industrial, commercial, scientific, academic, voluntary, or part of the public sector? What are its objectives? If you are a consultant or an information broker, or if you are employed on some other independent basis, perhaps you work regularly in different types of organisation. Even if you have not done any freelance work, your career may still have taken you through several of the categories mentioned.

Organisations, as well as being grouped under broad headings relating to purpose and objective as above, are also classified according to their structures and control systems. Over the years they have been the focus of numerous research studies, out of which a variety of differing theories have emerged. In the early 1960s the work of Burns and Stalker was seen as a new way of looking at organisations, concentrating as it did on the way in which industry attempted to manage innovation. More recently, their book on the subject was re-issued, Burns and Stalker (1994), and is still regarded as proposing a valuable way of considering the success of various management methods, particularly in today's climate of rapidly changing economic, social and especially technological conditions.

In their original study they looked at the influences which determine whether different types of management are successful or not. One particularly interesting section sets out two management systems, mechanistic and organic, which represent the extremes of control, authority and communication operating in organisations. This provides an instant picture of the potential impact of organisational type on personal development. It shows clearly the differences in communication processes, i.e. one-way or two-way; the degree of hierarchy; and the opportunities for employee involvement and development. Although these represent the opposite ends of a pole, and many organisations are likely to fall somewhere between the two, it can be seen that certain characteristics make an organisation much more flexible and able to adapt to rapidly changing situations.

Senge (1993 & 1994) also looks at the organisation from the point of view of its management style and structure. He focuses on companies which develop their ability to learn and to absorb new ideas and practices at all employee levels, thus gaining competitive advantage. Teamwork and shared vision feature well up the agenda as they do in those organisations which have a strong and successful knowledge management policy.

The working environment: its influence on the information service

The organisational setting in which we work has a very powerful influence on the way in which we view our jobs, and possibly other aspects of our lives. The physical environment, as well as the management style, will contribute to the level of job satisfaction. Improved physical working conditions can bring about considerable change in staff attitudes, an increased sense of organisational 'belonging', and positive cohesiveness, where little may have previously existed. This in turn leads not only to increased productivity, but also to less quantifiable benefits for the organisation; for example, individuals from Company A will talk positively and enthusiastically about their organisation to those in Companies B, C and D. Through such exposure Company A may gain an enviable reputation among other companies - and possibly some new clients!

If your employing organisation considers that a good physical working environment is important, you are likely to have support for creating an attractive and workable library or information centre, which will contribute significantly to both use and user- satisfaction.

The size of an organisation, as well as being seen as a determinant of structure, has direct implications for the way in which information can be provided, both in terms of ease of access and speed of delivery. If your organisation is housed in one compact building and there is a central collection of information resources, easy access and quick delivery should not be too difficult to provide. If, however, there are a number of separate sites to be served and/or there are several separately located physical collections to be exploited, the process can become more complicated, even with electronic access either to a central listing of the total information resource, or directly to the sources themselves. If not thought through carefully at the planning stage this could lead to frustration being experienced by both users and information staff. This is where interaction between the organisation and the librarian or head of information is essential, not just when the service is being planned, but at all times, so that the most appropriate service continues to be given and changes made as appropriate. Such interaction takes place in a variety of ways. For example, membership of certain internal committees presents you with a ready-made forum where ideas for possible change can be floated, and feedback sought. This is especially useful if the new service that you wish to provide could possibly be linked with a development in some other part of the organisation, thus bringing about dovetailing rather than duplication or incompatibility. Such consultation is particularly important when the purchase, hiring or leasing of equipment is involved, to ensure compatibility as well as gaining agreement on the allocation of expenditure.

In the case of a multi-site organisation, or one with several information points, compatibility of systems and software is essential if a cost-effective communications network is to be maintained, although of course this is also dependent on personal interaction, both formal and informal, as well as technological systems. The physical location of information resources plays a big part in determining the amount of use made of them directly by enquirers. But in some organisations all or most of the use will be by the information specialists themselves; there may be few personal visits; therefore location is of secondary importance. This is often the case with specialist research departments where information work does not centre on responding to enquiries, but in acquiring, analysing and presenting information to management. The work is mainly proactive and is likely to be an ongoing part of the company's planning process. In this case user response is likely to be based on the quality of the analysis, the final presentation of the information, and its timeliness to management, rather than the comprehensiveness and ease-of-use of the information centre by enquirers.

Feedback is not easy to come by, except in the case of extremes - there will always be a response to an outstandingly bad piece of work! Sometimes acknowledgement will be made of work that is excellent; rarely is there feedback on the very satisfactory remainder of the continuum. So if you want to know whether you should continue a particular service or launch a new one you will have to seek a response and monitor success. For example, when Sylvia Webb first joined Stoy Hayward (now BDO Stoy Hayward), a leading firm of chartered accountants with at that time over 600 staff, (now considerably larger), the diversity of enquiries suggested a need for a weekly in-house business newsletter. To find out whether that really was the case, she compiled and circulated four issues over a period of one month. Each issue had a brief return slip on it, asking recipients to indicate the newsletter's usefulness to them. The enthusiasm of response was overwhelming, and continued to be so with take-up not only within the London office, but also from associated offices and others who expressed an interest. Apart from the basic considerations of coverage, length and presentation, all important, what are the implications of this example for personal development? Below are listed some of the advantages experienced from this project.

(a)   It provided a direct communication channel between the information staff and each user, as well as offering the opportunity for regular interaction with other staff not normally direct users of the service, e.g. secretaries passing on requests for further details of items included in the newsletter; clerical staff distributing material; and printing staff who produced the multiple copies.

(b)   It provided an essential reason for information staff to maintain a continuing interest in the organisation's and the individual user's business activities, and helped form a comprehensive base from which a whole range of other information requirements could be identified and satisfied in terms of resources and services.

(c)   It required information staff to keep up to date with business developments in the outside world by regular scanning of the press.

(d)   It heightened the information staff's awareness of the relationships between certain interest areas so that those could usefully be grouped in the newsletter for speedy reading by the user.

(e)   It involved the use and development of such skills as discrimination (i.e. selecting only the relevant items), writing, abstracting, time management and meeting deadlines (e.g. it was much quicker to use a dictaphone than to write if you were passing on the work for someone else to input, and word processing (still in its early stages at that time) with the facility of setting up a standard template, really cut down on editing time, as well as offering a more flexible means of organising the content and improving the presentation. The newsletter was issued every Monday, thereby creating deadlines, not only for its production, but also the administrative procedures involved.

(f)   It had positive implications for teamwork and motivation among information staff, e.g. shared monitoring of the press (today this would probably also include relevant websites and newsfeed services), shared follow-up to responses, shared awareness of information requirements, as well as a feeling of direct contribution to the organisation's business.

(g)   The processes involved were able to be incorporated into various parts of a staff training programme.

(h)   It enhanced the role of the information manager and staff in terms of the use of both management and information skills, and resulted in increased recognition of the individual and the information service as a valuable and vital part of the organisation.

You might find it helpful to itemise the personal outcome of any developments in which you have been involved. It can be a most constructive exercise leading to greater awareness of the implications of such developments, both for yourself and others involved.

What has just been described is but one example of how improving the service can at the same time offer opportunities for personal development. One of the outcomes noted above, namely (b), is of course something that should be taking place from the day that the individual joins the organisation and will come about in different ways, both active and passive. For example, where a formal induction to an organisation takes place, the individual will be given information without having to seek it.

The induction process

The induction programme may vary in format from company to company, but its purpose will be the same; to familiarise the new employee with:

- the organisation: its different departments and functions
- the people: putting names to faces and establishing who has responsibility for what
- the surroundings: what is where, from the cloakroom to the chief executive's office
- the job: precisely what the new employee is going to do, why, where and with whom.

The induction process falls naturally into four stages with stages 1 to 3 taking place on the first day.

Stage 1

A discussion with Human Resources or Personnel staff at the start. This is likely to last about 40-60 minutes and will cover the nature of the organisation and its work in general terms, as well as the precise details of the conditions of employment. The new employee will be given an opportunity to ask questions and seek clarification. At this stage a general outline of any formal training programme offered as part of the job may also be discussed, although this could be an area which the personnel officer would leave to the head of the department in which the new member of staff will be working.

Stage 2

A detailed discussion with the head of department describing the department's specific function and its relationship to the organisation as a whole; the style or approach adopted by the department; the other staff in the section and how they relate to each other; the particular job and responsibilities of the new member and any training arrangements. If there is to be a formal training programme it is best to set up a separate meeting to discuss this in detail. At this stage personal introductions will be made within the department and the physical layout, range of sources and various IT systems and other equipment explained. It is important that the new employee be made to feel part of the department as quickly as possible by being able to relate to the people and the place, e.g. having a desk prepared before their arrival with appropriate stationery and perhaps an in-tray labelled with their name. Once they feel they have a personal base from which to work and to which to return, they can move out into the wider realms of the organisation. It is also important to mention such things as lunch arrangements, e.g. when to go and where the in-house dining facilities are or nearest/best sandwich bar is located. Arrange for someone to have the same lunch hour on the first day so that the new employee can go out or to the company restaurant with someone who 'knows the ropes'.

A first day should not consist only of introductions and guided tours. This is the time to establish what the job itself is all about. If you are the manager, you should ensure that the new recruit has some specific tasks to carry out, say for the whole afternoon. This will give them the opportunity (a) to understand more fully what sort of work is involved, (b) to feel part of the department; and (c) to have the satisfaction of being active rather than passive. They will then feel a sense of achievement from Day One. Further aspects of the manager's role in developing his or her staff will be discussed in Chapter 5.

Stage 3

A tour of the building with introductions to key departments and staff. These should be kept brief at this stage - it is not easy to absorb a great number of new faces and places at any one time. More detailed knowledge will occur on a gradual basis through the work process.

Stage 4

The formal induction day. This may coincide with the newcomer's arrival or may take place some months later, depending on company policy. In some organisations these occur only once or twice a year, in others they are arranged for each individual or whenever there are enough new recruits for a group programme. They may include all new recruits at whatever level, or may be aimed at certain groups, e.g. new graduate trainees, new managers.

Such induction helps the new recruits to begin to understand the organisation as an integrated whole, and to see how their specific role slots into place. As time progresses they will also be able to understand more fully how best to carry out their work so that it makes the best possible contribution to the organisation. An excellent short guide to the induction process is produced by the UK's Advisory, Conciliation and Arbitration Service (ACAS) (2001) in their advisory booklet series, which looks at a range of employment issues. The titles are listed on their website *www.acas.org.uk* with brief summaries of the coverage. The series is updated regularly and is well worth looking at.

However, not all organisations operate an induction programme, and some may do so only once or twice a year. As a new employee, particularly if you have been appointed to set up or expand a library or information service, you will have to initiate a process of information gathering, to find out about the organisation, its structure and activities, and how and where it operates. This exercise should be followed by a detailed information-needs analysis. Checklists for this purpose can be found in Webb (1996a) *Creating an Information service.* (Although published several years ago, these should still be useful, and will help towards getting you to feel part of the organisation, as well as establishing what it does and what it needs.) It is essential that you are fully aware of management's expectations of the information service from the start, so that you can assess the skills as well as the resources required to meet them. As you become more familiar with the organisation and identify other needs, so you will create further expectations to be fulfilled. In the early stages it is essential to plan carefully, to manage and control the service's development. Do not try to offer everything at once, everything may not be appropriate - and what will you do for your next trick? Trying to do too much at once can actually lead to a low level of achievement in terms of both the service provided and job satisfaction, not forgetting the longer-term health implications. Time, or lack of it, is often seen to be a major problem, particularly in small special libraries, which may be one-person libraries, and especially in the setting-up period. This is when the use of appropriate techniques, such as time management, can be extremely important (see Chapter 5).

To return to the organisation, its commitment to staff development is as important as that of the individual. Without support or encouragement of one sort or another from the employing authority, the individual could find it difficult to achieve his or her personal goals. Company policy on this varies tremendously, but there will usually be some means by which personal development can take place. Where the objective of an organisation is one of education or training, it is highly likely that staff development is not only encouraged, but expected. Of course, there are always exceptions, but usually the type of organisation just mentioned will actively encourage the individual to pursue personal growth. Naturally it will still be on the understanding that this will be of definite benefit to the organisation in some way, but from a personal viewpoint this does add purpose to the activity.

Ashridge Management College, already mentioned in Chapter 1, is a good example of this type of organisation. During Webb's time there all library staff received positive support for various kinds of personal development. Library assistants without formal qualifications were encouraged to attend short courses and seminars and to study for the appropriate City and Guilds Certificate on a day-release basis. Support was given for a member of staff to pursue a two-year course at the City University. This was also on a day-release basis and led to a Diploma in Information Science. Qualified staff were encouraged to study for further degrees, carry out research and attend management courses. The college paid all the fees and expenses involved, but this was seen as an investment in (a) an improved information service, and (b) satisfied and highly motivated staff who were likely to make valuable long-term contributions to the college. Librarians in similar organisations have also reported receiving the same sort of encouragement, although in some cases it has been from an individual rather than the organisation itself. This can pose problems when the individual mentor moves on; it is not always easy to find a replacement.

At Ashridge considerable emphasis was placed on employee involvement. Staff in all departments and at all levels were encouraged to participate in the staff consultative process and to serve on various committees and working parties. There were also social activities involving both staff and course participants. Generally there was a feeling of personal involvement in the College's activities, rather than one of just 'going to work'. Such staff involvement is of course vital to any independent organisation, especially one which is self-financing and does not receive regular funding from external sources. Such organisations are dependent on generating ideas for the growth and development of the institution from within, and this requires staff who are fully aware of and committed to its objectives and policies, as well as being innovative and highly motivated.

Educational organisations are usually supportive of developmental activities as they relate directly to the organisation's own objectives.

Case study 1

J. Eric Davies at the time of writing holds the post of Director of LISU, the Library and Information Statistics Unit based at Loughborough University, and is an excellent example of someone who has spent a long time in one organisation, but has certainly not stood still. Anyone looking at Eric's CV cannot help but be impressed by his qualifications and numerous publications and research activities. But these have only come about through the constant pursuit of knowledge and skills, an innate inquisitiveness, a need to know and a desire to learn, and as he emphasises, through the consistent support that he has had from his employing organisation and his colleagues. His interests are wide-ranging: from data protection to benchmarking and performance measures, from research techniques to budgets and general management.

Eric sees personal development as a continuous lifelong process, saying "I have always had a desire to learn more and master new skills and techniques. I've been lucky to get opportunities - but I have also made the most of them. CPD (Continuing Professional Development) doesn't work unless you have a passion for what you're doing at the moment, a belief and commitment to what you and your organisation are trying to achieve, and a willingness to extend yourself just that little bit every day."

It is this awareness of being part of the whole organisation, and wanting to participate in the achievement of its overall aims and objectives that provides these opportunities. Eric continues, "I have been fortunate in having had some very good mentors (though they didn't call themselves such) and at least tacit support, often more, for undertaking all sorts of CPD related activities such as committee membership, research and writing, studying for additional qualifications etc. A term's study leave to write a book was a singular example of visible institutional support. When I became an academic, it was, of course, a 'given' that I would pursue scholarship - an expectation that I relished.

I have also had the benefit of working with energetic and enthusiastic colleagues who were equally keen on behaving professionally and pursuing CPD. Many have gone on to take on a variety of key roles. The resulting atmosphere was one where mutual professional stimulus and support prevailed whilst at the same time we could challenge each other's thinking in a 'safe' and constructive context.

But it isn't just in terms of career progression that I judge my success, or otherwise. I have enjoyed the interaction with fellow professionals on committees etc. and made some wonderful friends. I have also acquired lots of new insights to people, places and processes. You can't buy all that!"

Eric also notes the importance of putting something back into the profession at large. One example of the way in which he has pursued this is through taking on the role of Vice-Chair of the Library and Information Group (LIRG) at what is seen as an exciting time. The group is soon to be assimilated into the UK's professional body, the Chartered Institute of Library and Information Professionals (CILIP) . This role has involved considerable work in constitutional re-drafting as well as handling the mechanics of assimilation. Eric finds this work very rewarding and says that it provides proof that "what you put in is returned several fold in terms of professional stimulus, expanded horizons, knowledge and genuine fellowship".

In a different type of organisation, especially a large one, there may be less emphasis on employee involvement in the decision-making process but just as much support for self-development. This may be through formal training opportunities for staff at each level of the organisation; cross-functional management development programmes and short courses being a common combination in both the public and private sectors. Alternatively, individuals may be encouraged to make proposals according to their specific needs and make use of in-house training provision, in order to utilise the considerable knowledge and experience of the existing workforce and to provide cost-effective training on local premises.

In some companies there may be arrangements whereby the company will pay certain course fees, with the individual buying books or other related material. Attending a course may be seen as acceptable, while participation in less formally organised external activities may not. However, it is generally felt that representation of the company at meetings and conferences should be regarded as a public relations opportunity for the organisation, as well as a means of development for the individual. It also provides a valuable network, through new contacts made, for the exchange of information. Study leave or time to study during the working day is offered by some firms, usually as part of formal training leading to a professional qualification. Membership fees to professional bodies are also often paid by the company, if the membership relates to the professional skills involved in an individual's work. Some companies provide other more general educational activities, such as language classes in the lunch break. Staff training and development may be the function of a separate department within a company, or a function of the Human Resources or Personnel section, or the responsibility of individual heads of departments. Wherever this function falls within the organisation, there should operate mechanisms whereby the individual and the organisation, or more specifically its representatives, are able to interact and communicate their needs and objectives, so that these may be met by the most mutually beneficial means. Appraisal interviews, counselling sessions, committees and staff meetings are the most common settings in which such interaction takes place. If used properly, with the necessary follow-up action, these provide excellent vehicles for two-way communication.

Whatever form the training and development programme takes, it can still achieve the same end, providing a means of communication across as well as within functions. In the LIS context this can also result in valuable feedback to information staff about how the information service is perceived and how it is meeting other departments' and therefore the organisation's needs. In most industrial and commercial organisations, as in others, the management decision to invest money and resources in an information service is made not in isolation but with the intention of improving the profitability of the company as a whole. A performance assessment of the service will need to be made by the use of appropriate measures and over a period of time. Measurement could be based on the analysis of various types of user response to the delivery of specific services, e.g. current awareness bulletins; searches for particular projects, asking questions about the form of delivery, timeliness, appropriateness and comprehensiveness of information, and above all how useful the information was in contributing to the particular business activity. The aim therefore is to ensure that the total service is as appropriate, efficient and cost-effective as possible.

This approach can involve the use of the client/user interview, or survey, considering particularly the user's evaluation of the service. This may be by quantitative or qualitative methods; the key point being to gather enough relevant data to allow analysis, using well-structured survey tools. Crawford (2000) describes these with case studies in his excellent book on evaluating LIS, and discusses performance measures for the electronic library. Benchmarking, by which organisations measure themselves against others - traditionally "the best" in the field - has long been carried out at an organisational level, but until fairly recently its use by LIS to measure their own performance has not been as widespread, nor taken place in all sectors. However, more recently tools have been produced to help in the process, and this could certainly present a field for further personal development, as well as an opportunity for evaluating and enhancing the service. This is discussed further in chapter 8.

Such evaluations and assessments will not only highlight any need for change and development in the service, but should also be considered as providing valuable indicators of direction for the individual information worker. Personal development can then be viewed not as an end in itself, but as something which will best be achieved where organisational and individual objectives match or are complementary. The process and its outcomes are not just job-specific, but will have long term benefits for the individual undergoing it and for the employing organisation. Further discussion of the implications of organisational culture on self-development takes place in chapters 5 and 8.

References

Advisory, Conciliation and Arbitration Service (2001)
Recruitment and induction. London: ACAS

Burns, Tom and Stalker, George M. (1994) *The management of innovation.* Oxford: Oxford University Press

Crawford, John (2000)
Evaluation of library and information services. 2nd edition. London: Aslib

Senge, Peter (1993)
The fifth discipline: the art and practice of the learning organisation. London: Random House Business Books

Senge, Peter (1994)
The fifth discipline fieldbook: strategies for building a learning organisation. London: Nicholas Brealey

Webb, Sylvia P. (1996a)
Creating an information service. 3rd edition. London: Aslib

Chapter 3

Starting your career

So you have decided to become an information professional! You are in the last year of your studies or perhaps you have already completed a degree or diploma in librarianship and information studies, or in information science. What next? How can you decide on the programme of action most suited to your personal needs and ability? This will require not only careful thought on your part, but also well planned action.

A simple start would be to think back to the reasons that made you embark on your course of study in the first place, and to look through any material that you collected at that time. If this has been filed away for a while, you will need to update your information, so that you are sure that you are considering all the current possibilities and data. A lot of useful careers information is available on the Chartered Institute of Library and Information Professionals (CILIP) web site, and those of the various schools of information studies, e.g. the RAGU site for London Metropolitan University (formerly the Universities of North London and Guildhall) has links to a number of useful web sites in education, training, and employment. If you are still in the process of carrying out your studies, your personal tutor, or the college or university's careers officer, should be able to help, by discussing the different types of information work available, and helping you decide to which you would be best suited. Most universities and colleges are happy for their students to continue to seek advice from the Careers Advisory Service after the course of study has been completed, and at later stages of their careers. Prospects, the UK's official graduate careers website, has a section on career planning and you can give yourself a psychometric test to discover your ideal career. The Prospects site also provides details of graduate market trends: useful if you want to check the average starting salary for an information position! There are also a number of independent career consultants, who can be traced through the website of the Chartered Institute of Personnel and Development (who maintain a list). This list, at the time of writing, is slightly difficult to find: from the home page, go to 'Events' and select 'Forums' from the drop-down menu. Within Forums, select 'Counselling and Career Management' to access a Directory of Career and Outplacement Consultants (in pdf format). Alternatively, you can check with any of the careers associations listed in *Directory of British Associations* (2000).

Types of information work

In an increasingly global job market, with opportunities opening up for much wider transferability of professional skills, it is essential that you are realistic in recognising your particular strengths and the gaps in your knowledge and skills. This is important when deciding on the type of information post that you would not only like, but to which you could also make the most effective contribution. That same job market, however, may not produce what you have in mind at the time, so it is essential to draw up a profile which will indicate to you the widest range of jobs into which you would fit. It is likely that, as part of your course, as well as during the vacation periods, you will have worked in one or several different library or information settings, and will have carried out a variety of tasks. Even so, you will not have been involved in more than a small percentage of what is now potentially available to you.

What kind of work is involved?

In spite of all the technological advances of the past few years, any information service will still involve the same basic activities: collecting and evaluating information, recording and organising it, retrieving and communicating it when needed. In addition, any service must be designed, marketed and managed.

- *Collecting information* may mean buying published documents or assembling company records or gathering data - from a wide range of sources. The relevant information must be selected, evaluated and perhaps summarised or abstracted.

- *Recording information* means describing and indexing it so that it can be readily retrieved, by compiling lists or catalogues which may be printed or stored in computerised form.

- *Organising information* involves storing it so that it can be easily retrieved when needed. This could mean deciding how to arrange books on shelves or how to structure the way information is held in a computer file or database.

- *Retrieving information* can involve a wide variety of sources - hard copy directories, books and journals, specialised online databases, personal consultation with experts etc.

- *Communicating information* could involve, for example, compiling regular briefings on new publications about a specific subject, arranging for electronic alerting services or presenting oral market research reports on particular products.

- *Designing information or knowledge systems* to solve particular problems involves systems analysis, computer programming, web or intranet development.

- *Managing information systems* may be concerned with managing the total information flow within an organisation, or with the management of an information unit or library.

- *Marketing and promotional activities* may include carrying out user surveys or conducting focus groups, and using every opportunity offered to raise the profile of the information service.

Finally, in a fast-changing area such as this, there are openings in research, training and education.

One feature of the last several years has been the growing convergence between the tasks associated with 'librarianship' and those of 'information science', and latterly, knowledge management. The broad headings above can encompass a huge range of tasks, each needing particular sets of skills. Some snapshots of the work involved are given below:

•Responding to specific requests for information, by identifying and searching relevant information sources, and evaluating and presenting the results to the enquirer. The sources concerned may be held 'in-house' (in documentary form, as records in a database, or as human expertise), accessed online or via the Web, or be located outside the organisation - perhaps in a business or technical library run by the public sector, or in an information unit of another similar organisation.

•Anticipating needs for information, on the basis of informal or formal studies of expressed needs by individuals, and through regular discussions with the organisation's management as to the workings, goals, and ethos of the organisation as a whole. Such work may involve initiating the transfer of knowledge on a regular basis as new material enters the system, via current awareness services directed at general audiences and/or by regularly despatched alerts or new material directed at individuals, and highly targeted in terms of subject content.

•Undertaking the preparatory work associated with document (and information) storage and retrieval. Such work may include, for example, down-loading document records into a local database prior to reformatting them for inclusion in an information bulletin, writing abstracts for reports written within the organisation, assigning keywords, metadata or classification codes to documents, inputting commands so as to keep in-house databases up-to-date, ensuring the document collection is up-to-strength and properly maintained, and validating information.

•Undertaking systems analysis and design so as to improve the systems which handle internal and external information resources. This might, for example, include the development of guidelines or methods for the use of local or wide area networks to ensure that information resources are available wherever needed rather than limited to discrete areas within the organisation; or regularly reviewing procedures so that their effectiveness and efficiency are maximised.

•Implementing commercial intelligence systems which ensure the efficient collection of information on competitive activity. Information input to such systems may well require vetting, and sources of information require constant redirection, to secure an inward flow of adequate, valid and relevant data. You will also need to be up-to-date on copyright and licensing issues. Pedley's Know How guide (2000) gives clear guidance on these matters for library and information workers.

•Providing specialist input (in association with other professionals in the organisation) to the development of databases of expertise, best practice and other knowledge content. Some examples of this might be carrying out a knowledge audit of the organisation, or building a taxonomy of its information and knowledge assets.

•If you are working in a public library environment getting involved in reader development initiatives, or those geared to Lifelong Learning or which target issues of social exclusion. Whatever kind of information service you are working in, you are likely to be involved in improving, through training, the 'information literacy' of service users: enabling users themselves to retrieve and evaluate the information they need more efficiently.

•Compiling plans for the future development of the service, and tenders for external funding, perhaps as a member of a consortium. An example of this might be tendering for funding for a major digitisation project.

•Representing the service internally on project and other groups, and externally on professional committees, benchmarking and other groups set up to exchange best practice ideas and measures.

•Carrying out regular evaluation, at the managerial level, of the scope and priorities of the service, in association with users. Further to this, links between the information service and external information-providing agencies will need to be assessed and developed.

Finally, note that the successful carrying out of information work involves not only working where the necessary specialised sources are located (i.e. within the library or information unit) but also getting out and actively meeting the people whose needs provide the *raison d'être* of the service.

The role of professional associations in personal development is discussed in more detail in Chapter 8, but there are important points to be considered in relation to the personal qualities needed for various types of information work. As the job involves close liaison with users, to find out their information needs and to feed results back to them, a pleasant outgoing personality is required. The job frequently involves working to time deadlines, so the ability to work accurately under pressure, without panicking, is essential. In smaller units, librarians and information officers may well be working in isolation from any fellow professionals, so independence and resourcefulness is helpful. To enable the service to develop, initiative and an enquiring mind are also required. For those in charge of other staff, some knowledge and experience of management techniques is essential.

It is well worth asking yourself what *employers* need and are looking for by way of specific attributes. A research study by Goulding et al (1999) found that a key quality sought by employers was 'innovativeness', that is, being open to new experience and having the ability to transform information about new concepts for personal use. Essential personal qualities deemed to be lacking in information staff include being:

* committed to organisational goals
* friendly
* able to accept pressure
* reliable
* energetic
* flexible
* logical.

You have been warned!

To return to the work setting, this varies widely, with increasing opportunities in the private sector. If you want a quick survey of these, just browse through the jobs advertised on *lisjobnet* or in the back pages of *Information World Review*. There are the traditional roles in a variety of settings: librarians and heads of information in advertising agencies, banks, insurance companies, stockbrokers, accounting and legal practices, management consultants, publishers, a whole range of industrial companies, professional and trade associations, government departments, schools, universities and colleges, and public libraries. You will also see some rather new or unusual roles advertised: a customer services librarian; a countywide information skills trainer; a sports development officer; a learning resource adviser; a product research analyst. Each of these will serve a different clientele, organising and exploiting a number of information resources in a variety of ways. Therefore the tasks that you may be required to carry out could vary tremendously.

Fieldwork carried out as part of your course is seen as making a valuable contribution to long-term career development. The Department of Information Studies, University College of Wales, Aberystwyth regards it 'as the indispensable link between the student's formal studies and the working environment' and continues in its web-based module handbook, *Work Placement*, to describe the educational, practical and professional benefits to the student. It emphasises fieldwork as 'a means of gaining some insight into the challenges with which library and information managers are faced in achieving objectives with other people'. Obviously this is something which will be of personal value to you, long after the formal studies have been completed. In the light of your work experience to date, return to Exercise 1 in Chapter 1 and consider the tasks listed there. Then gauge your response as suggested in Exercise 2. Another useful area to explore is transferable skills: the skills you learn from job to job or acquire at home or school. Sutton (2000) gives some helpful advice on identifying and evaluating these. Bryant (1995) also emphasises the importance of 'portable' skills, particularly communication (oral, written and working in groups), human resources management and interpersonal skills.

By now, you should be a little nearer to recognising the sort of organisation in which you would like to work, and the areas in which you would like to specialise. The latter may be a subject area, e.g. medicine; it may relate to the use of a particular professional skill, e.g. classification, indexing, reference work, or could be concerned with certain technical aspects of information work, e.g. intranet or web development. As well as taking note of your abilities and interests, and your work experience, you may also be influenced in your choice by hearing practitioners speaking about their jobs in specific fields - although their style and method of presentation will colour the picture. Discussion with your contemporaries about their fieldwork can also be helpful, but bear in mind that such views are not always objective, and your own response to a situation could be different.

The best way to assess your response has to be at first-hand. If you already have a clear idea of the sort of job you would like, why not seek out some appropriate organisations and approach the Librarian or Head of Information? Ask if you could visit their library or information centre to discuss the type of service that they operate. This may be arranged initially via your tutor or careers advisor if you are still at college, or through someone known to you who has contacts in your field of interest. Visits to see information services in action are valuable at all stages of a career; they are part of the continuous learning process and can provide a source of inspiration on all aspects of organising and handling information. At a later stage in your career you might be involved in setting up a new collection, or evaluating some software, or developing a training programme. Discussion with someone already working in the field will always prove a great help, so you might as well start setting up professional contacts now. They are a vital part of your long-term professional and personal development.

If you have not yet obtained a postgraduate qualification, you may be looking for a one year training programme especially designed to provide practical learning experience.

A well-structured training programme with the guidance of an enthusiastic supervisor can offer untold long-term benefits in terms of personal development, way beyond the formal objectives of such a programme. The following example illustrates the type of programme that could be on offer if you are seeking a one-year placement before moving on to postgraduate study.

Example: Graduate training scheme

Dorothy Faulkner, Director of Academic Services at Dartington College of Arts in Devon, regularly employs a post-graduate trainee on a one-year graduate training scheme (formerly referred to as a pre-library-school training programme). Dorothy and her staff note that there are considerable benefits not only for the trainee, but also for the library and information service as a whole. Below is the framework which has been prepared for the one year programme and could be used for any other new members of staff who might be employed in the library and learning resources centre, although the complete training activity contains a great deal more detail than can be included in this example.

Dorothy and her staff have also kindly agreed to share their thoughts on the outcomes and benefits as follows:

Of the framework Dorothy notes that "obviously some of the items covered are "local", and even the major tools/philosophies of librarianship and information science are introduced through practical use of our existing systems and working methods."

She is a strong believer in the value of practical experience and feels that her own career was much richer as a result. She says "As my own career initially developed through working as a library assistant and studying librarianship at evening classes, the opportunity for postgraduate study arriving much later, I still wonder how much less comprehensible and rich those studies would have been without the foundation of practical experience and knowledge."

Dorothy also notes the value of practical training in providing skills which could be used outside, as well as within the library/information field, saying "We hope that for the trainee this [the one-year programme] provides not only a real experience of information work, but also the opportunity to acquire transferable skills useful to those who eventually may decide not to undertake postgraduate study [in this field]". Of course, those skills would be equally useful to add to the knowledge gained through postgraduate study, especially those concerned with building up an understanding of how to interact with a variety of people.

Lauren Bell, the current trainee at the time of writing (who has also had casual employment in public libraries before joining the Dartington team) says that the pre-library school year has:

- given her more practical work experience, which will hopefully deepen the learning experience on her library/information course

- given her new skills and areas of knowledge: cataloguing, customer care, legal issues such as copyright, and a clearer idea of how libraries organise information

- allowed her to make a realistic assessment of the positive (e.g. enquiry work/helping students) and negative (e.g. repetitive nature of some tasks such as shelving) aspects of a career in librarianship

- clarified the particular areas of librarianship she would and would not like to work in.

As the programme's supervisor/manager Richard Taylor says:

"I would add to these benefits some of my own:

- especially with a small team such as ours, a new trainee every year can help keep the team dynamic fresh

- a good trainee can provide an interesting new library dialectic, a bad one a challenging management issue."

Dartington College of Arts

Library and Learning Resources Centre

Training Framework for New Members of Staff

History/organisation: distinction between Trust and College, Academic Services, etc (see Staff Manual - Mission and aims, Management Structure)

Accidents and emergencies: panic button, qualified first-aiders, first-aid box, accident book, fire extinguishers, fire exits, fire alarm, etc.

Library layout: intruder alarm/keypad, lights, keys, quiet study areas, noticeboards, etc.

Telephones: list of internal extensions, how to make an external call, personal calls.

Arrangement of library stock: Why we use different classification schemes for different forms of stock: Dewey for books, in-house schemes for sound recordings and printed music. Basic principles of Dewey + filing suffixes, main sequence/stack sequence, current journals/ back issues, reference, music full scores/oversize, music parts, videos, records/CDs. Items temporarily put on reference are noted in the reference book so they can later be removed.

Customer care: try not to leave problems unresolved or difficult customers unsatisfied – pass to Deputy Librarian if unsure. Importance of a "professional manner".

Priorities: at the issue desk swift throughput of borrowers should be paramount (assistance with photocopying of secondary importance). Off the issue desk daily routines should be done first *i.e.* shelving, then processing books and journals.

Heritage: enquiry screen: Boolean logic, "wild card operator", differences between 2 search screens (advanced is the best option), how to recognise the different sequences on the computer.

Enquiries: encourage students to use the full range of our information resources in their research. If an enquiry is made simply because a student is unsure how to use [the] Heritage [library system] – offer some on-the-spot training! Printed reference works: general and arts specific. Online resources: library useful links page, abstracts and indexes, library catalogues (the British Library, Library of Congress), bookshop catalogues. If you can't help with an enquiry, always offer to pass it on to someone else.

Data Protection: privacy of borrower information on Heritage and the legal reasons behind this.

Copyright: fair dealing, licences held by the College (CLA, ERA, DACS), limitations on copying different media (books, journals, sound recordings, printed music).

Opening and closing procedures: alarm, power switches on computers, "Z" readings on the till, starting up/shutting down Heritage, tannoy announcements. Don't leave the counter without arranging for someone to cover for you. If absolutely necessary - e.g. in the evening - always lock the till drawer and take the key.

Photocopiers: loading paper, removing jammed paper, toner cartridges, advanced colour copying features.

Photocopy cards: how to charge them up, 25p for new cards.

Brown cards: issuing a new brown card (if uncertain of the person's I.D. ask to see their library card), how to take payment from a brown card, refunds can only be made at the end of the year.

Class materials: prices, storage, giving class materials to academic staff (they should have a green card but discretionary use of the class materials book for small amounts). Student requests for credit.

Till: different key settings (off, reg., refund, "z"), photocopy cards/class materials/phone cards, cheques (only accepted over £5), rectifying mistakes, loading till rolls, refunds.

Borrowers: student code of conduct, library rules regarding borrower behaviour, differences in maximum items allowed, length of loan period, whether they can make reservations, whether they can take out records/CDs /videos, whether they can use computing equipment, different procedures for joining the library (external borrower forms, etc), defaulters, *always* ask for I.D. if unsure of borrower's identity.

Heritage: issues, returns, renewals

Issuing/returning slides: boxes need re-cataloguing in the title field on issue and return.

Heritage: fines. How to take fines off someone's ticket (once paid!), how to make a part payment and waiver. If someone wants to know what a particular fine is for, click on the "Charges" tab; if they then want to know the titles, take down the accession numbers and cross-reference them with "History". We are normally prepared to let students with a fines debt take books out, although there will be a crackdown at the end of the year before the summer vacation!

Shelf-checks: used for books students would like to borrow but can't find; also for books reported returned and reported never borrowed. Next action taken if s/c unsuccessful: notifying students, replacement costs, how to trap lost books and reserve if found. Remain politely noncommittal with student's "I returned that books weeks ago" yarns.

Heritage: reservations. How to make reservations (easier from the enquiry screen - no need for acc. no. or ISBN), cancel reservations, and check a borrower's position in the queue for a popular item. What to do when a reserved item is returned (reservations tray). How to print the reservations letters (important to put the "collect by..." date, as well as the reserver's name, with the item on the reservations shelf).

Heritage: cataloguing. Basic principles of cataloguing: AARC2. MARC records and non-MARC compatibility of Heritage. Difference between control numbers and accession numbers. Using authority files. Practical experience in cataloguing.

Trapped items: check for messages in Accession Record. If unsure pass to Deputy Librarian.

Darkroom/PTC keys. Signing-in book: signing a key out, crossing it off on return. Students need a darkroom training certificate before they can be added to the list of users. Students wishing to use the PTC need to be on the PTC intranet spreadsheet (and ticked for the particular areas they are allowed access to).

Photocopy packs: reference only, kept for individual modules, any new items need a backup copy making.

New books. Opening book parcels: check contents against packing slip, send any invoices to Finance, put books on processing shelf. After cataloguing: stamp, label, tattle-tape, check for any reservers.

Processing journals: marking-up, tattle-taping, stamping.

Borrower requests for items not in the library: ILL limits for different user categories. Get users to include as many bibliographic details as possible on the ILL request slip, *i.e.* the ISBN, publisher, date of publication, etc.

Hi-fi equipment. How to record from CD/record onto tape/mini-disc (bearing in mind copyright restrictions!).

Information Technology. Word-processing (where necessary). Using

College e-mail (+ attachments, virus prevention). Staff intranet/student intranets.

Job-seeking

Having identified the direction that you want to take, where will you find such jobs advertised? CILIP's *Library and Information Appointments* (available in print or on the Web) is the most comprehensive UK source as it carries numerous advertisements for jobs at all levels and in a wide range of organisations. It appears fortnightly. The jobs columns of both local and national newspapers should be scanned thoroughly, particularly the weekly 'Creative & Media' section of the *Guardian*. The *New Scientist* is another source, as are the *Times Literary* and *Education Supplements*, although none of these carry large numbers of library and information jobs. Jobs in specific fields may be advertised in trade journals, such as *Campaign* for the advertising world (which publishes annually a Top 300 listing of advertising agencies – useful when finding out about a potential employer), or special pages in the national dailies - for example, the 'Legal Appointments' pages of *The Times* often advertise library and information jobs in legal firms. The examples given here are of UK press sources; if you are outside the UK, contact the national professional associations for suggestions of appropriate journals and newspapers. If you are looking for a job in the public or voluntary sector, it is worth checking *jobsgopublic.com* which is devoted to UK public sector careers.

There are also a number of specialist recruitment agencies, some of which offer a job search facility on their websites, as well as a range of other services to candidates. Before contacting an agency, you do need to have carried out some basic preparation in terms of assessing your own capabilities and career direction. Some ways of doing this are suggested above. Krechowiecka (2000) provides detailed guidance on using the web for self-assessment via tests of personality, aptitude, vocational interest and intelligence. If you have not used an agency before, you will need to do some preliminary research to identify the most appropriate one for your purpose: this market has expanded considerably in recent years, and there are now some dozen recruitment agencies that handle information appointments of various kinds. Details of some of the main agencies will be found in the Appendix.

Arrangements for candidates vary from agency to agency. Some of the longer established agencies such as Aslib Professional Recruitment Ltd and InfoMatch require candidates to complete a paper form which covers personal details, education, career history and work experience, with a detailed statement of proficiency in a range of technical library and information skills. This is submitted along with a CV prior to meeting an agency consultant for a discussion on your experience and aspirations.

Most agencies like to see candidates face to face (Aslib will conduct a telephone interview if a personal visit is not feasible). Don't despair if you live outside London and are seeking work elsewhere in the UK or overseas: many agencies have a regional presence, or arrange periodic visits to larger towns and cities. Sue Hill Recruitment and Services Ltd holds regular interviews in London, Birmingham and Manchester, and other interview sessions from time to time in other venues. TFPL (which has offices in the UK and the US) organises regional recruiting days in major cities, as does Instant Library. Instant Library also visits universities in England, Scotland and Wales to interview final year students seeking first professional posts: check their web site for details. Glen Recruitment on the other hand, who cover a wide range of posts in the information, library and knowledge sectors, focuses on recruiting in the London area.

It is increasingly common for candidates to approach an agency via its web site. Personnel Resources, whose information positions include researchers, planners, database analysts and information specialists, offer candidates the choice of e-mailing a current CV or filling in a form online. Glen Recruitment offers the facility to apply for selected vacancies online. Phee Farrer Jones, whose specialist areas include Research and Information, also offer a job search facility in Quick or Advanced mode. If you're a graduate and registered as a Phee Farrer Jones member, you can browse in the Job Shop and drop likely jobs into your shopping basket. You can also set up a job alert facility, and be e-mailed about likely vacancies. If you register with Price Jamieson, specialists in digital and marketing communications recruitment, you can save a number of job searches which you can re-run on the web or through your WAP phone.

It is also useful to check out what other services agencies are offering. Aslib, InfoMatch and TFPL provide free basic advice on CV writing and interviews. TFPL additionally offers various priced services including personal action plans and psychometric testing, whilst Sue Hill Recruitment runs workshops on getting jobs and coping with redundancy.

The agency or agencies you register with will all have their own strengths: InfoMatch sees its strength enhanced by its professional association (CILIP) backing; TFPL has built up quite a niche for itself in knowledge management appointments; Personnel Resources consultants are all specialists so have a good understanding of where candidates are coming from (and seeking to go). At the end of the day, you will probably settle with the one or few who put the most opportunities your way, or who seem to understand your requirements most clearly. You should always keep the agency informed about the outcome of interviews, including any arranged independently, and whether you wish your details to continue to be kept on file.

What should you look for in a job advertisement? Read it carefully; note what is expressed as an essential requirement - do you match such requirements, and does the job match yours? You may be looking for a job which will include a training programme to help you progress through CILIP's registration process. If formal training of this kind is available it may well be mentioned in the advertisement.

The costs of training may also be reflected in the salary scale. A well-structured training programme with the guidance of an enthusiastic supervisor can offer untold long-term benefits in terms of personal development, way beyond the formal objectives of such a programme. If, however, there is no mention of training, but everything else looks good, apply! The detail of the training programme is better not raised by the potential employee at the interview stage, unless initiated by the interviewer. You can always pursue the detail once you have received a firm offer; with or without formal training the job will provide valuable experience and could still count as part of CILIP's approved service requirement. It is worth remembering that employers who do not have staff with the appropriate qualifications to supervise such training may be willing to arrange for an external supervisor.

Co-operation between different types of organisation can also prove extremely useful in broadening the base of a training programme, as was found in the joint initiative taken by Sylvia Webb and Mary Casteleyn when working respectively for Stoy Hayward, the large accounting firm already mentioned and Westminster City Libraries, a public authority. Their respective trainees were able to attend presentations in both organisations and gain valuable insight into the objectives and operation of two information services which, although very different, could offer each other a new method of approach and a broader view of career potential. This scheme was found to be so useful that it was repeated over a period of 3 years.

Applying for a job

Having decided that a particular published advertisement is of interest, note any closing date and look to see whether further details are available or an application form required. If so, these should be requested either by telephone, e-mail or in writing as indicated in the advertisement. Do not send your CV at this stage unless specifically directed. If, however, the application is to be made as a direct response to the advertisement, your CV with an appropriate covering letter should be sent, but only after having gleaned all the information possible from the advertisement and all other sources of information that you can think of.

Finding out about a potential employer

1 . In general:

- Talk to colleagues.

- Visit the company's web site. (Organisations are increasingly using their web sites to post job vacancy information, so if you have identified specific companies you would like to work for, this is a good place to start.)

- Visit appropriate libraries including those of professional and trade associations.

- Search any subject files or databases, especially those giving press cover, to which you may have access, or search the archive in ft.com, the Financial Times web site.

2. If the job is with an industrial or commercial firm, there are other possible sources:

- Visit your local business library to consult specialist directories in the firm's market sector.

- Look at company annual reports, especially the sections giving a general overview of the company's performance, such as the reports of the Chairman and the directors. These are often made available on the company web site, and for larger companies try the free CAROL (*Current Annual Reports Online*) service. However, do remember that reports produced by the company itself will present only its viewpoint, so beware of possible bias. Company reports are also promotional tools.

- If you cannot see the published report, you can access company details through the Companies House web site.

- Check not only directories such as Kompass (which covers a number of countries), but also those of various chambers of commerce and databases such as ICC's Juniper which lists smaller companies.

3. If you are applying for a job in the public sector the following titles will complement your web searches. *Britain* [current year]: *the official yearbook of the United Kingdom,* and *Guide to libraries and information units in government departments and other organisations* will give you information about the work of UK government departments and a whole range of national and regional bodies; *Commonwealth Universities Yearbook* and *The World of Learning* between them provide worldwide cover of the academic world, listing universities and research associations, with the names of both administrative and academic staff in the various faculties and departments. *The Municipal Yearbook* gives similar information on UK local authorities.

The above list can only indicate, by selected examples, the range of sources available to you when seeking information about an organisation. The *Directory of British Associations* and its European counterpart, as well as *The Aslib directory of information sources in the UK* and *The Libraries Directory* will help you select further specific sources that may assist.

Presenting your application

Having carried out your research, and maintained your interest in the job, the next step is the application. This, whether made by form or by letter, will determine whether or not you get an interview. The application sets up a picture of you in the potential employer's mind, it represents all that he or she can know of your suitability for the job at this stage. Therefore it is up to you to present yourself in the best possible light. The first and most important thing to remember is to follow the instructions.

If it says 'use block capitals', 'applications should be typed', 'enclose a copy of your birth certificate - *not* the original', 'complete in ink in your own handwriting' - then do follow the instructions. Secondly, whatever the format, a tidy, clean, easy-to-read application is much more likely to be received favourably. Content and style are also important. Keep sentences brief but informative. Think carefully about each question on the form before deciding on an answer. Try to see it in context, in the light of your research and any information provided by the company itself. Read all details and the application form right through before putting pen, or keyboard, to paper. Make a rough draft of sections other than those requiring only names, dates and places. If you are able to copy the form and use the copy for drafting, it will improve the layout of your responses, and will act as your reference copy. Put yourself in the position of the person who will be reading (or more likely, quickly scanning) it. Does it emphasise what you need to emphasise for the purposes of the job? Are there gaps in the chronology that might raise questions in the recruiter's mind? There is usually a space for stating your leisure interests - use this carefully. If you have a great number of such activities, do not attempt to list them all. Select three or four which reflect the range - your potential employer is probably more concerned that you have outside activities as a balancing factor, rather than being interested in how you fill every day of the year, unless of course the activities indicate possible areas of conflict with the organisation's objectives.

The final section of most application forms invites you to volunteer 'any other information'. Again, be selective. Include any professional activities; work experience that has been of particular interest, any special skills; and - if there is no separate section provided - why you are not only interested in, but also suitable for this job. Quite often a covering letter is requested as a statement of your reason for applying.

If no application form is available, the same general rules apply, but this time you have to choose the content and its presentation, so make the most of it. This is best in the form of a standard CV which you can use for each application, accompanied by a covering letter which will vary according to the particular job under consideration. The CV should be kept to two pages of A4, if possible, and word processed. Figure 4 suggests a possible layout and indicates the details to be included. Some of these may be considered optional, e.g. age. (Note that as your career progresses, the Education section can drop all reference to schools attended and your schools exam results, and may usefully drop down the CV to switch places with your career history. Likewise, your career history will contain more detail for your most recent appointments, with anything over 10 years old restricted to dates, job title and employer).

The covering letter should be kept to one side of A4. It is better not to use smaller notepaper as A4 is a standard size, it can easily be filed by the recipient, and stands less chance of getting lost! It also gives you more room to set out your statements. This should be prepared as a business letter, with the name and address of the recipient at the top, and a heading showing the post applied for, with any reference given in the advertisement. If there is a personal name, then do use it rather than 'Dear Sirs', which was the traditional way to address an organisation, but is now regarded as being sexist. If there is no personal name, it is quite in order to write 'Dear Personnel Manager' or whatever title is suggested in the advertisement.

Figure 4: Suggested layout for a curriculum vitae

Place headings on the left, underlined or in capitals to make them stand out, with information underneath and in line. Use double spacing between items to help them stand out. Do not use too many different type faces as this can distract from the content.

Items in square brackets [] on the example which follows are an indication of content and not to be included as words on the CV.

CURRICULUM VITAE

NAME *[in full]*

HOME ADDRESS *[include telephone number, mobile number and e-mail address]*

COLLEGE ADDRESS   *[include telephone number, any College e-mail address which you have established can be used for student contact and the date to which this address will be valid (if you are a student)]*

DATE AND PLACE OF BIRTH   AGE

NATIONALITY

EDUCATION AND TRAINING

1. SCHOOLS (Secondary)

[Dates. Name and place of school(s).]

2. FURTHER AND HIGHER EDUCATION

[Dates. Name(s) of institution (s).]

QUALIFICATIONS

[Dates. Exams passed with grades, in chronological order, covering secondary, further and higher education. Give examination grades only if they are good. Always give class of degree. Mention any scholarships and prizes you have won as well as any other academic awards or research grants obtained.]

TRAINING COURSES UNDERTAKEN

[Date and course title of relevant professional training, e.g. European Computer Driving Licence]

PRESENT APPOINTMENT

[Date of commencement: job title and employer, when applicable, or simply 'student' and your college's name.]

PRESENT SALARY *[It is not always necessary to give your present grade and salary to an employer. Perhaps tell them in your covering letter what starting salary you would expect or wait until you are called to interview, and discuss it there. (Although you may need to declare this on an application form)]*

PREVIOUS APPOINTMENTS *[in reverse chronological order]*

[Include vacation work]

[Date of commencement and leaving with month and year: job title and employer]

SKILLS AND EXPERIENCE

[Summarise under sub-headings, e.g. supervisory experience, language skills, level of computing ability, public relations, driving licence and experience, and name the jobs in which such experience was gained.]

MEMBERSHIP OF PROFESSIONAL ASSOCIATIONS

[Title of association]   *[Dates, position, etc.]*

PUBLICATIONS

PERSONAL ACTIVITIES AND INTERESTS

[List with dates, positions of responsibility if you have been involved with any clubs or societies, etc.]

REFEREES *[usually two]*

1.*[Name with academic qualifications]*

[Title]

[Address]

[Telephone number]

[e-mail address]

2.*[Ditto]*

Example heading for a covering letter.

> Your address, telephone number, e-mail address
>
> Date
>
>
> Mr M. Ployer
> Human Resources Manager
> Company X
> 8 Job Street
> New Horizon
> Postshire NH1 3MI
>
> Dear Mr Ployer,
>
> **TRAINEE INFORMATION OFFICER - REF. XZ7.**

If you address this to a personal name, end the letter with 'Yours sincerely', otherwise use 'Yours faithfully'. Do use your first name in full, as well as your surname, when signing. It is much easier to identify with John or Mary Smith than A.N. Other. If your covering letter is handwritten then make sure that it is legible, especially your name! As with the application form, a preliminary draft is essential for both your CV and the accompanying letter. When you read it through, try to be objective. Read it with the job description and the recipient in mind. If you have a colleague whose professional ability you trust, ask for his or her reaction. Do not undersell yourself, but on the other hand do not make claims which you are unable to fulfil. In other words, be realistic, and keep all communications businesslike, avoiding irrelevancies. Think about each word that you use - is there a better one? When you are satisfied that you cannot produce a better letter and CV, then draw it up in the final form and check it thoroughly before signing it and putting it in the post. For some further practical guidance on job applications consult Sutton (2000).

Keep copies of all applications. These will be useful in several ways. Firstly, if you are called to interview you can check on what you have already told your potential employer. Take a copy with you to the interview for reference purposes. Secondly, you have invested a considerable amount of time in the preparation of your application, why not re-use some of those carefully-thought-out phrases, where appropriate, in other applications? Thirdly, it is worth keeping all applications in a long-term career file; you will then be able to check whether you have ever applied previously to a particular company. Fourthly, if you are not succeeding in getting to the interview stage after a number of attempts, perhaps you should review those earlier applications, as well as your personal checklists.

Making an application takes time, but it is an excellent investment. A well prepared application is likely to secure you an interview, which could lead to your first 'permanent' appointment. It is here that you will really start your development as a professional, not only putting into practice the concepts learned through your formal studies, but also observing and assimilating management at work.

But first get that job! Work on your interviewing techniques - they are necessary on both sides of the table and will be used continuously, in different ways, throughout your career, as is described in the following chapter.

Printed References

Britain [current year]: the official yearbook of the United Kingdom. Norwich: The Stationery Office [annual].

Bryant, Sue Lacey (1995) *Personal professional development and the solo librarian.* London: Library Association Publishing.

Commonwealth Universities Yearbook. 4 vols. London: Association of Commonwealth Universities [annual].

Directory of British Associations (2000) 15th edition. Beckenham, Kent: CBD Research.

Directory of European Industrial and Trade Associations (1997). Beckenham, Kent: CBD Research

Directory of European Professional and Learned Societies. (1995) 5th edition. Beckenham, Kent: CBD Research [updated edition in preparation 2003].

Goulding, Anne; Bromham, Beth; Hannabuss, Stuart & Cramer, Duncan (1999) *Likely to succeed: attitudes and aptitudes for an effective information profession in the 21st century.* London: Library & Information Commission.

Guide to Libraries and Information Units in Government Departments and Other Organisations (1998) 33rd edn. Edited by Peter Dale. London: British Library, Science Reference Library.

Krechowiecka, Irene (2000) *Net that job! Using the World Wide Web to develop your career and find work.* 2nd edn. London: Kogan Page.

Municipal Yearbook. London: Hemming Information Services [annual].

Libraries Directory, 1998-2000 (2001). Cambridge: James Clarke & Co Ltd.

Pedley, Paul (2000) *Copyright for Library and Information Professionals* 2nd edition. London: Aslib

Sutton, Brian (2000) *Job search: finding jobs and securing interviews*. London: Industrial Society.

The World of Learning. London: Europa Publications [annual].

Website References

Jobs and Careers. Chartered Institute of Library and Information Professionals. www.cilip.org.uk/jobs_careers/careers.html

CAROL: Company annual reports online. www.carol.co.uk

Companies House. www.companieshouse.gov.uk

Financial Times. www.ft.com

Lisjobnet: online library and information recruitment advertising. Chartered Institute for Information Professionals. www.lisjobnet.org.uk

London Metropolitan University: RAGU. www.londonmet.ac.uk/ragu/links.cfm

Prospects: the UK's official graduate careers website. www.prospects.ac.uk

Work placement. Department of Information Studies, University College of Wales, Aberystwyth. www.dil.aber.ac.uk/dils/modules/handbooks/IL30710/INDEX.HTM

Jobsgopublic: the UK's leading website for public sector careers www.jobsgopublic.com

Chapter 4

The interview as a focus for personal development

The interview exists as a mechanism through which formal structured communication concerning a particular problem or requirement can take place, with the objective of resolving that issue. Communication is two-way, with information being given and sought by both parties. It may involve two individuals, an individual and a group, or more than one group. The situations can range from the recruitment of a new employee to the identification of an individual's information needs, as in the library reference or enquiry interview. As such the interview can be viewed as an analogy for many other work situations in which you may be involved, all of which require the use of interpersonal, communication, and organisation skills. So, in that light, why not take the interview as an example, representing the many types of daily interaction you are likely to have, and apply the findings to that wider range of work situations?

Interviews are made up of individuals who assume roles, i.e. that of interviewer or interviewee. These are conducted according to various social rules, depending on the type of interview. However, there are two underlying rules which apply to both roles and in all types of interview. The first relates to preparation. This has already been considered from the job applicant's viewpoint in the previous chapter. Its importance to both interviewee and interviewer will be considered further as each type of interview is discussed.

The second fundamental rule concerns good manners. By the latter I am not referring to the use of 'please' and 'thank you', or shaking hands as you say 'good morning'. The interview is an interaction between individuals with the aim of attaining a solution . The participants need to be able to listen to each other patiently and objectively; exercise tact and discretion; and make decisions based on fact rather than opinion. Sarcastic comment, implied criticism, condescending remarks, or the exhibition of a self-important manner are forms of negative behaviour, and will not result in a successful conclusion of the interview.

How do you set about acquiring the appropriate interpersonal and management skills that will help you in the interview situation, either as a potential employee or as a manager seeking to recruit successfully? The first thing to do is find out about the different types of interview in which you could be involved at work. If you have recently completed your formal studies in librarianship or information science, you are likely to have looked at interviewing, and in particular the recruitment interview, as part of the management section of the syllabus. Perhaps you have already been involved in role-playing exercises aimed at improving your skills in this area. These provide a particularly useful means of learning. Further reading of some of the very practical texts on the subject will also help, for example, *Great answers to tough interview questions*, Yate (2001). Now in its 5th edition, this book quotes the *Financial Times* as saying that it is the best book on job-hunting. It gives considerable practical advice on all aspects of the interview and preparing for it, ranging from techniques aimed at getting called to interview, to the role of body language and appropriate mode of dress. There is also advice on negotiating your salary (another internal interview), and for a later date, on preparing to climb the career ladder. This book will be as useful to those seeking their first job as to those seeking to move on to a more senior position.

Although many of the management books about interviewing skills have been written with the interviewer in mind, they are equally worth reading by the potential interviewee. They offer a means of becoming familiar with the whole interview process, and help create an awareness of the general expectations of the interviewer. It is also worth looking out for any courses or career advisory sessions which might help, whether you are likely to be the interviewer or the candidate.

What are the main types of interview in which you might be involved at work? Those common to the whole organisation can usually be grouped under five headings: recruitment; performance appraisal; counselling; disciplinary; termination. They could all be broadly described as employment interviews, i.e. relating to aspects of an individual's employment. Apart from the first category they are all internal interviews, i.e. all participants are members of the organisation. Policy varies as to which interviews are carried out by a representative of the Human Resources or Personnel department and which by section heads, directors or others. As well as the five categories mentioned above, there are two types of interview specifically designed for use in the library and information context: the client or user interview, as mentioned in Chapter 2; and the reference or enquiry interview, discussed in Chapter 6. The purpose of the client interview, usually carried as part of a survey, is to elicit user responses to services. The responses can then be analysed and contribute to any overall service evaluation, providing data on which changes or improvements can be based.

The reference interview seeks to establish an enquirer's specific information need on a given topic and at a particular time. Longer-term these can usefully be followed up by analysis, this time of information needs. These may be analysed, for example, by subject area or by departments or functions.They may also be considered within time spans which will assist budgeting, for example, a project with a stated end-date may well need specified information on a daily basis, but only for a limited period of time. This will determine whether sources which may be useful in the future are actually purchased, or whether tailor-made information is bought in from an external source just for the duration of the project. So the reference interview can lead to the need to take a number of management decisions, all of which will require relevant skills and knowledge, illustrating how the process of personal development in information work can cover a wide spectrum of activities and perhaps lead you in unforeseen but rewarding directions.

The following discussion aims to introduce the purposes of the various types of employment interview and by doing so to highlight the personal skills that need to be developed. It must, however, be emphasised that more detailed reading is essential, and should be pursued in conjunction with other practical training in order that such skills may be acquired. Throughout this chapter the interview is being used as a focus for considering the broader area of interaction at work.

Recruitment interviews

The purpose of such an interview (commonly referred to as the selection or recruitment interview) is to make a major contribution to the process of selecting a person for a job. This is achieved by the exchange of a great deal of information about the individual, the job and the organisation, some of which will have taken place before the interview, i.e. information about the job and the organisation will have been passed to applicants via the advertisement and additional material, for example, a job description and a company profile, which are likely to have been sent out with the application form. Internal applicants should be supplied with the same information as external candidates and treated equally. If you are an external candidate, methods of finding out about a future employer are discussed in Chapter 3.

Completed application forms, covering letters and CVs will have presented the interviewer with initial details about potential employees. The selection process could involve a single interview or several. It may be on a one-to-one basis, i.e. one interviewer, one applicant; or individuals may be seen by a panel of people. There could also be participation with other candidates in the early stages of the process, e.g. presentation skills may be tested by the use of a role-playing exercise., or there could be an open session where a number of candidates meet selected members of the organisation perhaps for a general question-time, a tour of departments, or over lunch.

Some interviews include the use of occupational tests to assess a particular aptitude or type of personality. These should only be administered by persons holding certain recognised qualifications, usually in an area of the behavioural sciences. There have been numerous popular presentations on how to interpret social behaviour, but it requires a great deal of knowledge and skill to be effective, so leave it to the experts. The tests just mentioned should give no cause for alarm to the interviewee. If they are motivation or personality inventories, they are not 'tests' and therefore do not have 'wrong' or 'right' answers. They usually require the candidate merely to put a tick in a box to show preferences for various alternatives. These, analysed appropriately, will indicate what is most important to you at work, or how you would fit into the organisation in terms of working relationships. Such 'tests' do not require preparation beforehand, and are only one part of the interview process. They are also used in vocational guidance by some career consultants, as are aptitude tests which assess an individual's suitability for a particular type of work, e.g. working with computers.There are various other types of tests or analyses which claim to provide information about a candidate's personality and suitability for the job, but are certainly not all recognised or used by a majority of companies, e.g. graphology - the analysis of handwriting.

The dialogue of the selection interview is likely to follow a sequence, moving through the details on the application form to a discussion of the organisation and the job. This will be the substantial core of the interview, contained between the 'warm-up' (putting the candidate at ease) and the 'round-off' (thanking the candidate for coming and setting the expectation for the follow-up communication, e.g. 'we will be writing to you within the next seven days').

So what pointers for personal development does the recruitment interview suggest? The interviewer will require a whole range of management skills. These are as necessary in the pre-interview stage as during the interview itself, e.g. appropriate job specifications have to be drawn up before advertising the post, applications must be matched against them, and initial screening carried out. This increasingly involves checking with the awarding institution that a particular qualification is in fact currently held by the applicant. Prior to the interview, further reading of each candidate's details must take place, questions must be drawn up, and each interview prepared for. During the interview interpersonal skills come into play, e.g. there is a need to develop a sympathetic awareness of what the potential employee is likely to be feeling. Because the interview is important, he or she is likely to be more than normally nervous. So make allowances for this, and try to put the candidates at their ease. Nevertheless it is still essential for the interviewer to remain objective. Interpersonal skills are based on the use of good communication skills. For example, questions should be formulated so that they do not encourage 'yes' or 'no' answers, or indicate that there is a preferred response. Communication skills also involve listening, giving the candidate time to consider the question and the best way to reply. It is usually necessary for the interviewer to make notes; these should be brief enough for the candidate to feel that he or she still has the interviewer's full attention, and clear enough to communicate their full message back to the writer when consulted after the interview. In preparing, the interviewer should draw up some headings as a framework for the note-taking, and some key questions to be put to the candidate.

Legislation in the UK and elsewhere requires that any personal information written or communicated about individuals must be made available to them should they request it, therefore non-contentious language should be used in the interview notes, whether on paper or in electronic form. This is not new. For example, the UK's Data Protection Act of 1984 allows employees to see e-mails and other computerised records about themselves and this was extended to cover manual records by the Data Protection Act of 1998. There has since been further clarification of this whole area in the UK's Information Commissioner's subsequent code of practice on access to employee records. For further information on the way this works in the UK and also concerning the employee's right to know and consent to the transfer of such personal information to another country where their rights may not be as well-protected, it is well worth reading Ticher (2001).

Administrative and organisational skills are equally important to the conduct of the interview, e.g. preparing the interview room; ensuring that you will not be disturbed; and allocating enough time, of which maximum use should be made. If you are intending to involve other members of LIS staff in the interview, or in any introduction to the department e.g. meeting the other staff, giving a general tour of the LIS, ensure that they are fully briefed. Involvement of your staff will let them know that you value their contribution both to the process and to the final decision on the appointment. Leave enough time for a brief discussion with your staff after each interview, whilst their impressions are still fresh.

What areas of personal development could help the potential employee in the selection interview? For the interviewee the task is to make the best possible presentation of himself or herself as an appropriate person to fill the vacancy. This will be based on some familiarity with the organisation, achieved through the research mentioned earlier; appropriate qualifications; confidence in their own ability to do the job and possibly develop it further; and the ability to communicate such information skilfully during the interview process. Internal candidates should do their preparation just as thoroughly. Although you will know quite a lot about the organisation, make sure that you are up to date with general developments and policies. These could influence the way in which the LIS itself develops and therefore provide ideas for the post for which you are applying. Consider yourself in this situation. You have already shown some ability in this direction as your application has resulted in an invitation to interview. Now you have to achieve the next step through face-to-face communication. First impressions do count! It is not enough to appear well groomed and professional looking, you have to feel at home with the image that you are projecting. Part of that image is also expressed through the way in which you move or sit, your facial expressions and any other gestures which make up your non-verbal communication. While not becoming neurotic about it, you should be aware of this aspect of your behaviour and develop it appropriately. Both oral and written communication, to be effective, need to be clear, free of jargon, detailed enough to be informative and concise enough to avoid irrelevancies or repetition.

The interviewee should remain as objective as the interviewer in both the description of personal strengths and weaknesses, and in discussion of his or her current job and employer. Arrogance and lack of discretion are not good business recommendations, but neither are timidity and reticence. This ability to judge the right balance also applies to the degree of formality to be exercised. The interviewer, while perhaps appearing less formal than anticipated, may well see informality in the candidate as indicating either a lack of interest, or an assumption that the job is already theirs. Getting the balance right is essential for both the candidate and the interviewer and it is well worth reading one or two business books on interviewing techniques, especially those which consider both sides of the situation. Several are listed at the end of this chapter. You also need to be aware of the cultural differences likely to be experienced in different sectors.

The development of such skills is a long-term investment for anyone involved in the management of a library or information department. It will help you get the best out of all types of interview and is central to effective staff management, in which the performance review or appraisal interview can play a considerable part.

Appraisal interviews

The appraisal interview is as useful to the organisation as it is to the individual. It provides a vehicle for two-way feedback which could contribute as much to the development of the information service as to that of the individual whose performance is being reviewed. It also forms the basis for constructive staff relationships. What is the main focus of the appraisal interview? Stated briefly, it is one of review and preview. The individual's progress through the period since the last appraisal is discussed, and out of this the future direction and development of the individual can be assessed. Personal files giving details of progress, problems, achievements, course attendance and counselling sessions, if continuously updated, will prove extremely valuable in planning the individual's further development, and indicate general future staffing requirements. Through this process suggestions for improvements to the overall service will also arise. The appraisal interview should not be seen merely as a salary review. Its aims are to improve job performance, identify training needs, and, most importantly, provide the means whereby the individual can not only speak freely about problems and ambitions of which he or she is aware, but possibly identify others which may not previously have been apparent. This can help eliminate anxiety in the minds of both the interviewee and the manager, and improve understanding. Video Arts has produced a number of training packages on the subject of appraisal interviews, including self-study workbooks on disk as well as videos and other training materials. A presentation *How am I doing?* provides a useful demonstration of the appraisal interview in practice.

Appraisal is a process which brings about problem-solving by the clarification of objectives. As such the interpersonal and communication skills described as being vital to the selection interview are equally essential here, only this time the participants already know each other. Therefore, striking the right balance between formality and informality is extremely important, and such scene-setting is the responsibility of the interviewer. Again, preparation and time are crucial factors. The interviewee requires adequate time for his or her preparation and should be given a list of questions or topics for consideration well in advance of the interview.

Do not assume that the interviewee is aware of the purpose of the appraisal; discuss it when you arrange the date and time. Explain the use of the pre-interview checklist. Invite any preliminary questions which there may be at this stage.

The manager's preparation requires not only careful thought, but structured organisation of that thought, so that nothing is omitted from the interview. Points should be put down on paper with enough space for unobtrusive note-taking during the interview. Although some managers prefer to do most note-taking on a laptop computer, this is one occasion on which it is not recommended as it could cause the candidate to feel uneasy and may suggest that the interviewer is not fully engaged with the candidate. Examples of the types of headings which could be used for note-taking are given in Figure 5.

Figure 5. Discussion points for library/ information staff appraisal interviews

1 . PROFESSIONAL SKILLS

Enquiry work

- telephone
- face-to-face
- written (by letter)
- via e-mail
- with external, internal clients
- knowledge & use of sources
(print & electronic)
Classification & indexing
- includes knowledge of subject areas
Monitoring/Scanning the press
including SDI (selective dissemination of information) services

2. TECHNICAL SKILLS

- use of computers for administration,
  communication and information seeking
- use of other equipment e.g. video recording, projectors etc
- searching techniques
- web site design
- physical organisation of resources
- display work
- non-book material

3. COMMUNICATION SKILLS

- written e.g. correspondence, newsletters
- oral
- aural

4. ORGANISATION OF WORK

- note-taking
- filing, e.g. invoices, correspondence (applies to both paper &
  electronic records)
- file-clearing according to agreed criteria
- innovatory
- administrative
- time management

5. PERSONAL AND INTERPERSONAL ASPECTS

6. GENERAL REVIEW OF PROGRESS /TRAINING

Listening skills and objectivity should be strongly in evidence during the interview, but these must be backed up by the ability to respond quickly where solutions to problems need to be put forward at the time of discussion. It is essential to allow enough time to cater for unforeseen issues which the interviewee may wish to raise, but which he or she may not do if aware of time constraints; so a well planned diary is a 'must'. However carefully you prepare your staff's appraisals, too many in one day will not allow the follow-up consideration and documentation that should occur, nor allow you any head-clearing time. Adequate preparation by the interviewer makes it much more likely that each candidate will get a fair hearing, so techniques for switching off after each interview must be developed. Writing up the appraisal, even in draft form, will help you to see it as having reached a certain stage of completion. You will then be better placed to concentrate on your next task. Another method is to do something completely different, preferably involving a brief change of physical environment. By creating a change of both mental and physical setting, you will achieve a fresh approach to the next appraisal.

Timely follow-up is part of systematic appraisal. It requires the manager to assess both internal and external training or development opportunities which may be available, and to put any necessary arrangements into action. The manager therefore needs to keep up with what is happening in the field. There is also the continuing responsibility of obtaining feedback from the individual in the form of evaluation of any training in which he or she participates. The personal file kept by the manager on each member of staff is central to such follow-up.

For appraisal candidates the whole process is one of personal development and should be viewed by them as a valuable opportunity to learn about their own strengths and weaknesses, improve their job performance, broaden their range of skills, and contribute further to the organisation. It also presents the opportunity for improved or enhanced personal relationships within the department and the organisation for both interviewee and manager.

Working relationships are the central concern of the other three main types of interview common to the whole organisation, i.e. counselling, disciplinary and termination.

Counselling interviews

These take place either as a response to the identification of a particular problem, or as part of a continuous process, such as a formal training programme in which they are scheduled to occur regularly. They should certainly form an essential part of any long term training. The purpose of the counselling interview is to solve problems which may relate to work or to private life, and, by solving the problem, to improve work performance and relationships. Grievance interviews therefore also fall into this broad category. In some organisations the counselling function may be carried out by the Human Resources or Personnel department, but it is usual for the direct line manager to provide the first point of contact.

Although all interviews are of a personal and confidential nature, counselling interviews are particularly so. They involve admissions of inability to handle specific situations or tasks. This may be seen as failure by the person receiving the counselling and as such requires sensitive handling. The interviewer also needs to be aware of his or her own limitations, including lack of knowledge, and in certain cases may need to seek further assistance, perhaps from or via the Human Resources department. The problems will vary in degree of complexity, but each will demand the same degree of interest from the interviewer. Analytical ability can be used to great effect in breaking down a problem into manageable parts, thus reducing its size and seeming insurmountability. Open channels of communication are vital. The sympathetic ear, and halving a problem by sharing it, are key features of the counselling interview, as is a followup meeting to ensure that the agreed solution is in fact working. Discretion, patience, understanding and practical advice with continuing concern are the management abilities needed in counselling, and employees at all levels of the organisation should have access to counselling so that problems do not become blocks to individual or organisational development.

Disciplinary interviews

Perhaps one of the most difficult interviews to handle, in that it involves a role-change for the manager, the disciplinary or reprimand interview is necessary to ensure that all staff continue to meet the expectations of the organisation to the best of their ability. Its aim is not to punish, but to improve performance, prevent repetition of the unacceptable behaviour, and protect other staff from the results of one person's carelessness. This interview is likely to have a strong emotional undercurrent, but the manager directing it must maintain a cool, fact-based approach. The purpose is to illuminate the facts and solve the problem. The outcome should be positive; improving, not damaging, working relationships.

Emotions which may well be present in the mind of an employee being interviewed for a disciplinary matter could include resentment, anger, disappointment, loss of face, a feeling of being singled out unfairly for something which may have been regarded as common practice, and possibly above all a fear of job and income loss. There will also be concerns about how much is known by others in the department, or elsewhere in the organisation, about the reasons for this interview; and as a result, how the interviewee is likely to be regarded in the future by colleagues. Depending on the seriousness of the matter under discussion and the likelihood of dismissal, the response of those outside the organisation such as friends and family may also be important. The way in which these emotions may be expressed will vary considerably according to the individual's personality and general level of motivation and job satisfaction: whether they are happy in this particular work environment. Disciplinary matters may well be covered in a country's employment legislation and possibly have implications relating to human rights.

It is therefore essential that the manager is aware of such implications and strictly follows the disciplinary procedures set down by the employing organisation. A statement of the disciplinary procedures should appear either in the staff handbook or in the conditions of employment, usually given to new employees on their first day or sent with their letter of appointment. Seek the latest information from your personnel or human resources manager, who may also need to be involved in the interview, depending on the nature of the matter under consideration. It is the employer's responsibility to inform all members of staff of any changes in such procedures; the manager must ensure that he or she reads such communications carefully and understands the implications for both self and staff. The person being interviewed must also be made aware of their rights in this situation, including that of possibly having another person present during the procedure.

The whole interview must be based on facts; it is essential to prepare carefully, having checked all the facts before listing the issues involved, and to adopt a practical approach. The ability to get to the point quickly, present the facts clearly, achieve agreement that they represent the situation, and put forward proposals for improvement, whilst retaining the respect of the interviewee, are the management skills to be developed for the disciplinary interview.

The disciplinary interview may be one of several formal interviews which could lead to dismissal, which would be the most serious outcome.Therefore before conducting any disciplinary interview always check for any changes to the current legislation and company procedures.

Resolving the problem is much to be preferred both for the employee being disciplined and the employing organisation and the disciplinary interview can turn out to be a learning experience and lead to considerably improved performance and a more stable and happier work force. It may be that after an initial disciplinary interview the follow-up could usefully take the form of a counselling session. This will allow progress to be monitored and provide the opportunity for the employee and the line manager to discuss any continuing concerns. There are some excellent detailed checklists which will assist you in carrying out this type of interview in the section on Managing People in Rowntree (2000), which also covers the other types of interviews mentioned here.

Termination or exit interviews

When a member of the department resigns, for whatever reason, a valuable opportunity arises for feedback on the job that he or she is leaving. The termination interview provides an opportunity to look at the background to the resignation. It may be conducted by the departmental manager or the personnel officer. There could be implications for (a) the selection process, e.g. the appointment of staff over-qualified for the job, or the lack of promotion opportunities for those with a lot of ambition; (b) the conditions of employment, e.g. salary scales, holiday entitlement, the physical working environment, and (c) the department as a whole. However it could be argued that these are issues which should have been addressed earlier in the appraisal process, or perhaps have been discussed previously in whole or in part. That said, the information gathered at the termination interview will present the latest thinking on these matters and can be useful for future decisions. It could be used to review and improve the selection process and reduce staff turnover; or to solve specific organisational or departmental problems; and it will allow the leaver to feel that there has been a positive close to that period of employment. This is also likely to enhance the image of the organisation in retrospect, in the eyes of the leaver.

In handling such an interview the manager needs to be friendly, explaining how helpful such an interview could be for future staff planning; and persuasive, in getting the leaver to reveal additional facts behind the obvious reason for departure. For example, if the reason is one of promotion, it is useful to establish why promotion was not available within the present organisation. General comments and observations on a range of organisational policies and procedures are likely to arise out of a review of the individual's time with the company. Suggestions on the timing of such interviews vary according to company policy, with some carrying them out in the last few days of employment, others inviting the former employee back for lunch at a later date. This provides the opportunity to discuss the relevant issues in a more relaxed atmosphere, in which the lunch-guest has had time to reflect without the possible high emotions and frenetic activity which may fill the final few weeks of a job. This delayed termination interview may well generate a more balanced and helpful insight for the managers involved.

As well as acting on the points relating to the specific job which has been vacated, similar jobs, either in the same or perhaps in another department, might share similar problems. Feedback from exit interviews could usefully be shared with managers in other departments, perhaps as an agenda item at any regular management meetings, as well as being discussed with the human resources manager.

In the case of termination due to redundancy or dismissal, such an interview conducted by the line manager would not be appropriate; although in cases where a department has been closed down it has been known for the departmental or line manager to have to break the news. This would then need to be followed up by formal discussion and advice on contractual arrangements with the Human Resources or Personnel Manager, or another representative of the organisation, such as the welfare officer.

As with the disciplinary interviews already mentioned, all termination interviews must follow not only corporate procedures, but also legal and other regulatory requirements according the juridiction within which the organisation's operation falls.

Training for interviewing

The types of interviews described highlight the need for a broad range of interpersonal, communication and organisational skills; in other words those which make up the ability to manage people. It may be that your organisation arranges its own in-house courses for this purpose. If not, there will be quite a selection of short courses available externally. In the UK you will find these listed on the websites or in the printed brochures or directories of e.g. Aslib, TFPL, and CILIP and the various interest groups that relate to particular sectors or areas of activity(see appendix). Professional LIS associations and interest groups in many countries provide similiar courses.

However, interviewing is a general management function and you will find some useful courses being offered by management training firms with a broader remit. So wherever you find yourself working, it will be worth checking with the national associations or institutes of management in that country or region, as well as with business schools and independent consultants who offer short courses in interviewing techniques. Again each country is likely to have some sort of national listing of likely providers, perhaps in a general educational directory such as *The World of Learning*, or on the websites of national training bodies.

Choosing a course which suits your particular requirements will depend as much on company policy as on your preference. But it is worth sounding out colleagues and professional acquaintances as to which they have found useful and why. Considerations will be the duration and level of the course; its objectives and intended audience in terms of level and perhaps sector specialisation; location and cost. The training methods used are likely to be highly interactive and involve considerable exposure of the delegates in terms of having to participate in practical interviewing exercises which will either be recorded or watched "live" by the other delegates and the course facilitator and then subjected to constructive critical analysis. This is the part about which some course participants feel most concerned, but which in fact provides essential feedback from which the individual can learn and develop their skills and understanding of the interviewing process.

Closed-circuit television (CCTV) and video-recording are particularly useful in interpersonal and communication skills learning, so it is worth checking that such methods are included in the courses you select. There are also some excellent training films and distance learning packages which point out very clearly the differences between good and bad interviewing techniques. These are available for hire or purchase and are listed in the catalogues of the various producers, e.g. Video Arts; Industrial Society Learning & Development. Their addresses appear in the Appendix.

In using the interview as an example of interaction at work, it has been possible to point out the range of skills required to handle a variety of situations. This in turn identifies for you areas in which further personal development could take place. The skills described are not only relevant to the interview situation; they are the key to successful management and effective interaction throughout the organisation.

References and further reading

Edenborough, Robert (1999)
Effective interviewing. London: Kogan Page

Hindle, Tim (1999)
Interviewing skills. London: Dorling-Kindersley

Hudson, Howard (1999)
The perfect appraisal. London: Random House Business Books

Jones, Alan (2001)
Winning at interview. London: Random House Business Books

Rowntree, Derek (2000)
The manager's book of checklists. 2nd edition. London: Pearson
Education/Prentice Hall imprint

Shapiro, Mo & Straw, Alison (2002)
Tackling interview questions in a week. 2nd edition. London: Hodder and Stoughton

Ticher, Paul (2001)
Data protection for library and information services. London: Aslib

Yate, Martin J (2001)
Great answers to tough interview questions. 5th edition. London: Kogan Page

Chapter 5

Managing to develop

Good management is a main contributor to the health of an organisation, whether it be a public body or a privately owned company, and whatever its function. As far as the individual is concerned it is never too early to be aware of the management implications of a job, and their importance; nor is there ever a point in an individual's career at which this ceases to be a major consideration. The practice of any specialism is enhanced if it is consciously well-managed. Effective management is not a one-off operation with a beginning and an end, having a single, finite goal in view. Rather it is a continuous process of amplification, something that is constantly being built upon to increase its effect, and effectiveness, throughout the whole passage of a career.

Management involves handling resources and situations. In the context of an information department, 'managing resources' refers to the effective use of staff, finance, space and stock in its widest sense, i.e. information resources and related equipment. Managing situations entails setting-up and handling procedures, such as meetings and interviews, within a defined framework, making decisions and taking responsibility both within the department and outside it, in wider organisational terms. This is also discussed further in Chapter 8. Both resources and situations involve people. In the context of an information department the word 'people' refers not only to staff but also to users - anyone in the organisation, or sometimes outside it, is a potential user. However, it is important to remember that whatever type of organisation you work in, you need to think of people not simply as staff or as potential users of information, but also as colleagues or contacts to whom you relate in other ways.

Organisations have varying hierarchical structures, and accepted degrees of informality. Accordingly behaviour in interpersonal relationships varies. For example, you may behave less formally when discussing a matter among peers, than when reviewing a matter with a group of directors or other senior executives. The interaction between organisation and individual has been discussed in Chapter 2, but organisational climate and structure have considerable influence on the degree of control accorded to managers, and on the scope for entrepreneurial activity. If you want to read more on this, there are numerous comprehensive texts on the subject of organisational behaviour. These cover working relationships and management within organisations, as well as looking at organisations as systems.

The quality of the organisational communications network will influence the ease or difficulty with which employees can make a full contribution to the achievement of the organisation's objectives. There is also the additional communications need of each department or unit, which will relate to its function and objectives. Through the process of trying to meet both these needs, staff may experience satisfaction or frustration, thus identifying possible areas for personal development, which could also lead to the enhancement of organisational systems. In Chapter 4 the interview was chosen to illustrate the importance of interpersonal and communications skills to the manager. These are vital when you are in the information business, where you are the specialist, whose role is not only to organise, retrieve, and analyse information, but also to disseminate and communicate it both accurately and quickly. To do so requires developing a range of skills which you can use with confidence, knowing that they are appropriate to the organisation and the information service.

Meetings

Meetings behaviour also embodies these sets of skills and is certainly an area for self-development. A lot can be learned by observation - as much on what not to do as on positive behaviour. Remember that while each participant in the meeting may be waiting to put forward a view, he or she will not necessarily be listening to the person currently speaking. A series of monologues does not make a meeting. Two important considerations are control and structure. A good chair-person knows when to listen, and when to intervene. He or she will be able to assess whether discussion has gone beyond the agenda and whether it continues to be relevant or useful. This is where a well-structured agenda plays its part. It needs to be circulated enough in advance to give people time to consider each item, and to assemble any information which they intend to put forward for discussion. There is also an art in taking and writing minutes, particularly where the secretary is a participating member of a particular committee who has taken on the additional role of secretary. Therefore an efficient and knowledgeable meetings secretary is essential. *How to manage meetings*, Barker (2002), is an excellent guide to the different types of meetings in which you might be involved, and all aspects of their management, from writing the minutes to group dynamics.

The size of the group attending the meeting is another important point to consider when setting it up. The larger the group, the less detailed the discussion and the less specific the outcome is likely to be in terms of decision-taking. There is also the question of perceived status in being asked to attend, even if little contribution is anticipated. By some it will be regarded as a 'right', whether or not they have any useful input to make, by others an unpleasant duty, making them equally likely to be non-contributors. Meetings should be seen to have a purpose, and participants made to feel that their involvement is valued.

Meetings involve time, therefore money. They should be seen as practical mechanisms through which to address organisational issues and make decisions. They must be cost-effective, which is much more likely to be achieved if they are well-led and well-structured. The best way to learn more about meetings behaviour is to attend some meetings. As well as recognising their manifest purpose, you should also see them as valuable learning situations. Observe carefully the behaviour of participants, the role-playing and interaction. Meetings both inside and outside your own organisation will provide useful learning experience and help you improve the quality of your own participation.

Managing training

Managing is not just the concern of the departmental head. Every task that is carried out should be considered in terms of cost-effectiveness and professional performance by the person executing that task. All work has to be managed, usually to agreed procedures, so there are management aspects, whether task-oriented or people-oriented, to be considered by each individual, right from the first day of employment. Examples of these are indicated in the Dartington outline programme in Chapter 3, which also suggests a framework which could be used in any initial training, either as a basis for post-graduate training, or adapted and used at the start of any first permanent post. However, training and any other form of knowledge acquisition, form part of a long term career process. Therefore LIS managers will need to be able to develop long-term training and development programmes, both for themselves and for their staff.

If this is your first management post, it may be that you have not yet carried out much training yourself. However, you are likely to have attended courses and observed what makes for a successful outcome. There are also courses aimed at training the trainer, and numerous books about all aspects of training. *The Trainer's Toolkit*, Charney and Conway (1997), not only provides discussion of the different types of training with checklists and a variety of training tools to be used, but also covers training needs analysis and suggests a training cost grid which shows how to determine total costs of the training.

What follows is a discussion of the various considerations concerning training. From this you will be able to identify any areas for your own personal development as a manager and put this in the context of departmental training as a whole. Training and development needs will be different for each individual, as will their learning responses to different methods of teaching and presentation. The changing information needs of the employing organisation will also play an important part in determining certain elements of any training activities.

Information work particularly requires a subtle blend of skills, knowledge and understanding appropriate to handling both tasks and people in a variety of settings. An indication of the range of work and related skills is suggested in Chapter 3, and of course any specialist subject requirements or activities which form part of the LIS remit will also have to be taken into account. For example, subject-related requirements could be knowledge of a specific foreign language or the working of the European Community; there might be regular LIS activity carried out for other departments or as part of consultancy such as database construction and maintenance, website design and update. Some activities will form part of formal training and development, such as that required for professional memberships, others will be concerned more directly with service provision in a particular work environment, e.g. learning about legal or financial terminology if working in a law firm or an accounting practice; keeping up to date with current affairs in a government or business LIS.

The headings below might provide a useful framework on which to build such training and development programmes. What you include will depend on the specific workplace in which you are operating, so you may choose to omit certain elements and introduce others accordingly. However, the organisational and behavioural skills and techniques are likely to apply across the board. Scheduling will be a matter for individual judgement, but it is essential to include regular slots for feedback and discussion on progress. Some parts of the training may be continuous throughout the programme to allow new or more detailed aspects of a topic to be introduced in a timely fashion, or to reinforce earlier training. You may include guided reading to back up sessions - this is usually best provided at the time that an activity or topic is about to be introduced into the programme. You will then be able to offer the latest thinking on a subject, on which the trainee can build through visits to other organisations and attendance at conferences and seminars. Although you obviously have to bring in such activities as they present themselves, in order to take advantage of new ideas, that should not lead to training being carried out merely as a series of *ad hoc* events.

As a manager, you will need to ensure that anyone undergoing training and development in your department, has a clear idea of what is on offer and what the expectations are in terms of their commitment and performance. A well-structured programme which you can talk through with the individual will more than repay the time spent in designing it.

If the programme has been designed for a new member of staff the first section should cover the induction process as described in Chapter 2 and activities as outlined in the Dartington framework in Chapter 3. This will be followed by a gradual introduction to specific LIS policies and procedures, with the relevant training and feedback. For other staff the starting point would be a detailed discussion of the overall training programme, its rationale, objectives and methods; the main areas and activities to be covered; with a possible timetable. At this stage the person about to undertake the programme should be encouraged to respond to what is on offer and raise any questions.

Programme framework: suggested sections/headings

Apart from the induction process and training for staff new to the LIS field, more experienced staff who have been with the organisation for some time will have a different need. This is likely to be either the acquisition of additional knowledge and skills, or the updating of their current knowledge base and honing of skills already in place. Experience in designing such programmes suggests that the key areas in which training and development are most regularly required are the following:

~   skills and knowledge relating to new LIS activities generated by developments within the organisation e.g. knowledge management, consultancy

~   operational activities, particularly where an individual is taking on a new area of responsibility e.g. co-ordinating information involved through the stages of an administrative process such as the acquisition of material, from ordering through progress chasing to receipt and invoice handling

~   the enhancement of existing information and library services and related procedures and techniques e.g. ways of handling and recording enquiries, including evaluation of outcomes

~   implementation of change in LIS policy e.g. the introduction of fee-based services

~   the acquisition of advanced level knowledge in certain specialist subject fields, depending on the purpose and focus of the programme

~   computer-related activity

~   research skills

~   teamwork and staff relationships e.g. where LIS staff are to participate in a project, or will themselves be conducting some training

~   professional issues and current LIS debate

~   interpersonal and communication skills (spoken and written) relating to work activities, such as:

    - choice of appropriate approach in different situations(formal or informal, use of electronic communication or personal contact)

    - style and manner in telephone or face-to-face interactions, listening, clarifying by questioning, explaining

    - presentation of information, use of words and

> graphics, appreciation of clear layout, visual aids (all apply equally to printed and electronic communications)

~ management and organisational skills
(includes many of the above as well as the following)

- agreed standard procedures
- financial/budgeting/planning functions
- time management
- flexibility
- people management
- ability to analyse & make decisions
- delegation.

Everyone has to manage and organise their work to achieve maximum effectiveness. Different methods suit different people, but there are tried and tested ways of making some activities more efficient, even, or especially, paper handling (yes, there is still plenty of it about). There is a need for agreement on methods of work organisation allowing co-ordination so that work can be shared or smoothly handed on or taken over. For example, the absence of one member of staff should not mean that any enquiry on which he or she has been working necessarily has to be shelved. If the originator of that enquiry comes in during the period of absence requesting a progress report, agreed procedures should make it easy to establish the stage reached.

Training and development programmes can either be developed as a comprehensive long term plan, or as a series of shorter focused modules to suit various stages in an individual's development. These could be spread over a longer period of time rather than being run continuously, thereby removing some of the time constraint often experienced by both supervisor and trainee especially in a small unit.

The programme: other key considerations

When drawing up a training programme or selecting an external course, the LIS manager will need to consider:

- **the purpose**
  - ~ ensure the programme complies with organisational training policy and strategy
  - ~ establish the overall purpose of the programme in meeting stated organisational, departmental or individual needs
  - ~ set out the specific objectives to be achieved

- **the candidate**
  - ~ the level of knowledge and prior experience to date
  - ~ the degree of motivation to undergo training

~ how the individual is to be prepared for the training

~ any special personal requirements e.g. special seating, facilities to assist hearing; personal commitments which will affect scheduling or location

- **the schedule**

~ normal LIS provision should not be compromised

~ scheduling appropriate to the stage of development and level of activity of candidates, so that it informs their work and enhances performance of the tasks which they carry out

~ frequency with which training activities take place. Time must be allowed for assimilation and feedback before the next stage of training commences

- **the methods**

[Training may involve several trainers according to the type of training involved, e.g. the LIS manager, another member of LIS staff, someone from another department, an external trainer. Different types of training will require different methods supported by a variety of training materials. Below is a list of the most commonly-used methods. Other aspects are noted in Chapter 8]

~ self-training, personal learning (includes reading, personal projects and computer-based learning)

~ one-to-one (includes coaching)

~ group training

- internal/external

- departmental, LIS, general

~ on-the-job (task-specific)

~ interactive (electronic or interpersonal)

~ lecture/discussion

~ demonstration

~ practical exercises

~ role-playing

- **the venue**

~ size and layout of training area according to purpose

~ acoustics

~ furniture, equipment, power points, lighting, heating, ventilation, general comfort

~ interruption avoidance (noise, intrusion, distraction factors).

Whether you are planning to conduct the training yourself or using someone else for this, you will need to consider which methods of training, and related training skills will be most appropriate to a specific type of training. This is essential if the stated objectives are to be achieved and individual needs met.

Counselling and feedback

Feedback and follow-up together form a vital part of any training programme. The management skills required for successful counselling have been discussed in the previous chapter, and in the context of a training programme the counselling session will also include elements of the appraisal interview, i.e. those of preview and review. The trainee needs to be well-briefed on the requirements of each module of the programme and receive regular and constructive feedback on progress. A useful way in which the trainee can monitor his or her own progress, and note points for future reference, is to keep a diary or log throughout the programme. This will have further use at a later stage as evidence of experience and progress if the trainee pursues other vocational or professional qualifications. Professional associations or other qualifying bodies can provide details of their requirements, essential for the manager offering a formal training programme for that purpose. Discussion with others experienced in such formal programmes will be valuable and could lead to some form of shared training activity.

It is important that all staff in the department have a sense of involvement in the training programme. They should also be briefed and encouraged to participate. Their contributions will be valuable and the programme will not be regarded as being exclusive.

There is tremendous scope for personal development in the management field. The significance of interpersonal skills has already been discussed in Chapter 4, but the management of yourself and your work through techniques such as time management and the development of a systematic approach to all tasks is equally important. Forms and files, computer-based or otherwise, required for recording details of work schedules and statistics need to be set up so that, once in use, they require minimal input to make them of maximum use in matters of planning and control. Suggestions for such an approach to the handling of procedures and records, are given in *Creating an information service*, Webb (1996). The checklist approach used there provides a practical start to structuring ideas for action.

Managing budgets

Handling a budget is one area where interpersonal skills and a systematic approach come jointly into play. Negotiating and justifying expenditure, possibly to a committee, and particularly for a department or service where the costs may not be recouped, certainly requires considerable powers of communication and persuasion. There is an excellent section on negotiating in *The Manager's book of checklists*, Rowntree (2000), which sets out the ground rules, the preparation needed, the bargaining process, and offers some useful 'Dos and don'ts'. In doing so it opens up the whole area of such interaction, looking at both the presentation of ideas and facts, and the responses likely to be engendered, making it equally useful reading on meetings behaviour on which there is a separate section.

Managing budgets, Brookson (2000) discusses the importance of understanding and preparing budgets as well as the importance of instigating monitoring procedures. The successful negotiation of a budget is also dependent on having all the facts to hand to answer any questions which may arise. For example, if an increase in the periodicals budget is proposed, then figures showing price increases, such as those compiled by Swets Blackwells, could provide, along with other considerations, valuable justification for such an increase. These are published annually in *Update*, the monthly journal of CILIP, usually in the June issue, and are based on a survey of ten major countries (i.e. the country of publication) in five general subject areas. Useful additional data comes in the form of an accompanying exchange rate table, allowing comparison across the currencies of the countries covered. In addition to the figures published in *Update*, Swets Blackwells produces three other reports analysing prices of subscriptions which they handle. Other useful tables are compiled by the Library and Information Statistics Unit (LISU) at Loughborough University. LISU produces trend analyses of UK and US academic book prices each half year and publishes an annual statistical summary - LIST (Library and Information Statistics)- which is distributed as a handy pocket-sized folder, also via *Update*.

One method which can help in monitoring the budget is to devise codes to indicate expense items. Each purchase can then be recorded by its code, providing a continuing, up-to-date record of how much is being spent on which area of the service. Such recording, which can be used for manual or computerised systems, also offers a means of quickly checking whether a particular invoice has been passed for payment. This can then be linked with copy invoices which may be kept by the library or by the accounts section. Without such systems, tracing management information can be cumbersome and make planning and control of expenditure difficult.

Budget preparation, the organisation of control records and systems, and the production of progress reports, all provide areas for personal development, which may not at first be apparent. For example, if there is a regular requirement to draw up and present progress reports, the thinking and decision-making processes involved in doing so can also stimulate ideas for personal future direction, as can other administration processes.

Successful administration

Administration does not always have the same appeal as, for example, enquiry work and other people- or technology-oriented tasks. It calls for skills in which many information workers would seem to have had little or no training. But in fact the structured and logical approach required to analyse and answer enquiries, or to carry out research, could be seen as providing a very good basis from which to handle administrative duties.

Standard procedures need to be viewed as a vital part of good management by everyone in the department. Procedures need to be seen to have a purpose and to make a valuable contribution to the information service, by ensuring that time is used effectively and that information is organised for ease of use. One way of achieving this, which has been used in a number of LIS, is the development of a manual of procedures, whether paper-based or in electronic form, or both. This has been successfully used as a training tool, providing new staff with a source from which to learn about the way in which certain tasks should be carried out, and an instant point of reference for future checking. It can be useful for temporary staff and for those involved in job rotation, ensuring consistency. For this reason it also forms the basis of successful quality management programmes, which have at their core agreed procedures and methods of ensuring consistency of quality in all activities.

The reason for the manual's success in achieving the above-mentioned objectives is that it is seen to be of value to everyone in the department as a source of reference to which they have committed themselves, not least by their involvement in its setting up (another team exercise) and through regular contributions to its updating and maintenance. This involves looking at each task to see whether it is (a) still necessary and (b) being carried out in the most cost-effective way; it entails constant talking-through of tasks and methods, providing a vehicle for structured discussion among staff, thereby creating wider involvement than just that of a trainee and supervisor; and it can be linked to relevant sections of each module of any formal training programme. It also provides a source of development for the supervisor or manager in that he or she will also be rethinking the organisation of tasks, and possibly, restructuring them in the light of the various discussions which have taken place. The reason for having both electronic and paper formats is that a copy of the latter can be available on the desk for instant use alongside any computer-based application which may be in progress. The computer not only allows regular and quick updating, but also access to the manual by users throughout the organisation via the internal network. It is therefore even more important to consider arrangement, layout, and general presentation for both formats, to ensure ease of use and clarity of expression.

Since the coming of the personal computer (the PC), and the Internet, there has been a proliferation of software packages aimed at any willing user. They are still coming. It is therefore necessary to consider in which areas of administration and management you will find these most useful. As well as providing a means of accessing and interrogating your information resources, software really makes administration much easier and allows you to get much more out of the data. Libraries and information centres have just as much need to follow standard business practice as any other department or unit, e.g. in the production of letters, reports, financial records and statistical analyses. Before computers became part of daily life, such activities were laborious in terms of the time required to carry them out and the need for constant double checking; this is where the PC really brought a welcome change. With appropriate software and proper use high quality documents can be quickly produced, and complicated calculations carried out. If you regularly produce documents which require text manipulation (e.g. editing newsletters, amending reports, personalising standard letters) you cannot afford to be without an up-to-date version of a standard word processing function in a current operating environment, i.e. Windows at the time of writing. This is essential if you are to communicate and network externally as well as internally e.g. with other LIS managers, exchanging information via e-mail or participating in an online discussion forum.

Appropriately well-structured software offers the facility to index the stored data for future searching and retrieval, or for further updating or amendment, making for a considerable increase in productivity and therefore time management. The variety and scope of software packages is considerable, they can certainly streamline operations. Look at them carefully and check any evaluations which may have been carried out. These appear regularly in journals such as *Business Information Testdrive*, as well as being carried out by organisations such as the Centre for Information Media and Technology (Cimtech).

With regard to financial and related management activities e.g. record-keeping, budgeting and planning; as already mentioned and probably experienced by most readers of this book, the computer is an invaluable tool. However, it is necessary to move with caution in terms of software selection. Otherwise you could be in danger of installing, often as part of overall policy, applications which you do not need and which just take up space on the system. Make sure that you have what is needed to meet your management requirements, rather than the latest "gizmo" that has caught the eye of the IT department. You need to establish what you require of the system to enable you to do your job as a manager. In the LIS housekeeping context, ease and speed of handling, storing and retrieving records, with the ability to produce regular statistics and analyses as required, is likely to be more important than conjuring up snappy graphics. Of course you will need a graphics facility, but choose one best suited to your purpose. Despite the obvious attractions of the powerful facilities that are available within many of today's software packages, their acrobatic ability should not be allowed to obscure the fact that, in small-scale administrative operations, ease of input and retrieval of the information connected with those tasks, plus a statistics package, is possibly more important than attaining the furthest limits of IT sophistication. All the tools which you need to support your departmental administration are likely to be dictated by central organisational policy. However, if your departmental needs are somewhat different, make sure that these are taken into account.

Always ensure you have the latest version of any package. The computer is a miniature data-processing department on your desk; as such it should be able to carry out all your day-to-day administration more easily and quickly. So choose your software carefully, and let the computer release you to carry out your other management functions. As well as providing a means of rapidly searching for and accessing information via the Internet, and using that technology to build internal networks (intranets) and set up LIS websites, the computer has really proved its value as an efficient workhorse in the co-ordination and speeding up of administrative processes, and in what has come to be generally described as library housekeeping. If this is an area where you feel in need of guidance, then you could start by contacting one of those centres which specialise in the field, such as Cimtech, which is also mentioned in the next chapter. Cimtech offers a range of courses and conferences as well as consultancy and publications; contact details are listed in the Appendix. Making use of the services of such centres of excellence could prove to be a valuable long-term investment, in terms of keeping up to date with useful developments and making contacts, as well as providing a continuing source of advice and information. Check the Cimtech publications for some background reading.

One area which must be taken seriously is that of protecting your system against viruses. This will usually be something decided at organisational level, but also needs to be regularly reviewed. Make sure that your anti-virus application comes into action every time you go online, not just at set times.

Time management and planning

Managing your time effectively has spin-off for others in terms of job-enhancement, for example in giving additional responsibility through delegation, in using hitherto untapped skills, and in making yourself more available to your staff and others who have need of your time. Setting up systems that work, experiencing the ease with which information can be traced and extracted for instant use in management planning and other administrative areas, can produce a great deal of job satisfaction, as well as contributing considerably to effective time management. Therefore, in a library or information department where staff are interdependent and work as a team, joint awareness of, and joint action in time management as a technique involves logging and analysing the way in which time is spent, to ensure that the best use is made of it. If such recording is carried out on a regular basis by all staff it provides valuable information for work-scheduling and long-term staff planning. *Making every minute count*, Haynes (2000), offers a useful guide to using time effectively and includes time analysis forms and charts which can be adapted to individual needs. There are several short courses on time management available from Industrial Society Learning & Development. These have been designed with different needs in mind, e.g. for those who do not have supervisory responsibilities as well as for those managing teams.

Time management also plays a central part in action-planning and target-setting, which can help to put seemingly insurmountable amounts of work into perspective. For example, in a busy information department where the work centres on enquiries, other tasks such as processing new resources, although equally important, may fall behind. Updating press files (still seen by many as a very valuable instant browsing resource), preparing new acquisitions, computer inputting and the daily updating of looseleaf services (still preferred by some users in certain fields e.g. law), are common examples of tasks which may easily stockpile during busy periods. Time spent in keeping resources up-to-date, could result in time saved in completing an enquiry.

First an awareness of the importance of keeping the service up-to-date needs to be created. Then a logical look at the tasks is required, asking for example:

~   How long does it take to file, say, fifty press releases, twenty letters and invoices, or to process ten new books or journals?

~   Are such tasks interruptable?

~   Can they just as easily be carried out sitting at a desk, where you are still available to handle enquiries, as by standing at a filing cabinet?

Another longer-term question may be:

~   Could the overall layout be changed, or stock moved, enabling it to be used more easily and fully?

The answers to these questions should indicate that such jobs are manageable if you and your staff do not attempt in one assault to conquer a whole mountain (sometimes literally, as demonstrated by Michael Everson in Chapter 6), but rather chip it into smaller boulders which are much easier to climb over.

Limits are an important part of action-planning. If you feel that you are going to allocate only half an hour, or an hour, to a particular task, and then move on to another job, not only will you see the task as something with which you can cope, you might also work faster in view of the time limit. Sharing the job also helps. If two or three people are going to carry out a job, each doing an agreed portion during the day, again it can be perceived as being in manageable proportions. What about interruptions? There are likely to be many. Enquiries mean interruptions, and must always receive priority treatment. So what about the action plan? Work to it while you can, but if you get an urgent enquiry, concentrate on that and, when it has been completed, review your priorities and draw up a new action plan for the rest of the day - or until the next enquiry! Flexibility and adaptability are also vital qualities for the information worker. However many times you have to redefine your plan and reset your targets, you will find you still achieve more through having planned than by not planning at all. The planning process itself leads to reconsideration of the necessity of certain tasks, or perhaps to more cost-effective ways of carrying them out. Corrall (2000) offers a comprehensive handbook providing a valuable source of reference which the LIS manager can consult on all aspects of planning.

Planning involves structuring your thoughts, usually resulting in the preparation of proposals and progress reports. Rowntree (2000) has a useful section on writing techniques in which he reminds the reader of the key elements of effective writing, with some guidance on how to achieve it. His book is itself a good example of effective writing in the way that he presents information, clear and easy to read, but comprehensive. If you are planning a new or radically changed service you will have to prepare a business plan, setting out your objectives and what is required to achieve them. This must always be supported by clear evidence, i.e. facts and figures, as to why this is the best way forward, showing full resource implications and a timetable of targets to be achieved. Blackwell (2002) offers practical guidance in *How to prepare a business plan*.

Communication skills

Your written communications can result in an invitation to present your case to a board or a committee. If you have little experience in this field, or feel that you would like to improve your skills, there are a number of courses involving practical sessions with feedback. These offer the best means of learning, and the acquisition of improved communication skills will boost not only your own confidence in your management ability, but also that of others, whose perception of you as a manager will be enhanced. First investigate the possibility of any in-house courses. If there are none in-house, then there are a number of external courses from which to choose. Try any reputable training provider, who could be operating specifically in the field of LIS or in management more generally. Some managers will have plenty from which to choose, others may decide to send candidates to another country for particular courses. For example, courses that we have directed for Aslib in London have often attracted an international audience, which really enhances the exchange of ideas among participants. Alternatively Aslib, and other training providers such as TFPL, will run their courses in most international venues. Related courses may be offered as a series from which you can take up individual courses as required or choose to invest in the complete series. By following a suite of courses participants will come away feeling that they have had a good grounding in the subject, including the opportunity in practical sessions to test the techniques that have been put forward. The participative aspects of some courses, such as making a presentation, might seem daunting, but will make the real thing much less so. A short course offering practical work with feedback will be a valuable investment, both in improving your spoken and written communication. Selected organisations offering such courses are listed in the Appendix.

Communication, whether written or spoken, requires preparation. However experienced you might be, careful thought is still required for each presentation; for example, what sort of people make up the audience, what information do they require, and what outcome is anticipated by the presenter? As well as writing reports and speaking at meetings, you will also need to be able to present your service to potential users, clients, and other visitors, some of whom may be information professionals themselves. Again your approach will depend on the make-up and requirement of the audience, and the main point or points that you aim to make. Presenting the service requires subtle judgement as to the message that you most want to put across, and your personal style and image is very much part of that message. You represent the service. If you appear confident and competent, so does the service that you are presenting. Take full advantage of all the devices that the professional speaker employs, e.g. good visual aids, not forgetting that you are one of them! Above all, keep the talk brief and lively. Do not fall into the trap of telling your audience about the methods by which you organise the service - tell them about the service itself, what it can do for them, how it can help the organisation or the LIS community. *Fast thinking: presentation,* Jay (2001), is a small practical guide which covers: making your case and getting it across, structure, visuals, the use of language and scripts. It is particularly helpful for those who suddenly find themselves in the situation of having to make a presentation at short notice.

Motivation and managing people

Underlying the individual's approach to all the tasks that make up his or her job, is motivation. Differences in personal motivation will relate to what he or she needs most from the job, e.g. for some the overriding need may be job security, a particular level of income, or a guaranteed pension.

For many people the work environment and interaction with colleagues are most important. Some will have specialist interests in a particular subject or business sector, while opportunities for career advancement and ambition fulfilment in specific functions top the list for others. Status and recognition are also needs to be met, as well as compatibility with private life. Some needs will be long-term and relate to the individual's basic personality, while others could change according to the organisational environment in which the individual finds himself or herself, and the balancing influence of his or her private life. For example, the individual may achieve the needs of status and recognition through social or leisure pursuits, or through involvement in broader professional activities outside the organisation.

For the manager, the word 'motivation' should give rise to thoughts not just of his or her own needs, but also those of the staff members for whom that manager has responsibility. Well motivated staff will achieve results - in this case a dynamic and effective information service with satisfied users - as well as experiencing job satisfaction. An important feature of being a manager is to exhibit the leadership qualities which will inspire and motivate his or her staff towards these results. Different styles of leadership will be appropriate to different types of organisation and situation. There are numerous management texts on leadership, but *Leading your team*, Leigh and Maynard (2002) offers a lot of practical advice. It considers how to be an adaptable leader, how to run team meetings and briefings, inter-team working, and virtual teams, and explains team characteristics and the support of team development. Action tips and tasks are suggested. Fisher (2000) considers the transition from supervisor to team leader in *Leading self-directed work teams*. Although in many general management texts examples are taken from commercial or industrial settings, the problems discussed and the ways in which they are handled are equally relevant to other types of organisation and offer as much food for thought to the manager of an LIS as to that of any other function. The approaches to control systems, positive thinking, and how to perform are essential to anyone who has to manage. The Chartered Management Institute, in conjunction with the publishers Hodder & Stoughton, has produced a useful series of short guides introducing many different areas of management. The "In a Week" series would be particularly helpful to the new manager, or to someone taking on a new area of management responsibility. Examples include *Business plans in a week*, Maitland (2002), *Web marketing in a week*, Gabay (2002), *Project management in a week*, Brown (2002) and many others.

Many of the decisions that a manager has to take concern other people, who may be seen as "different" or others who are not always easy to get on with. If you have to deal with such situations it could be worth looking at some of the Video Arts wide range of training films and packages, such as *Not my type: valuing diversity* or *Dealing with conflict*. Contact details for Video Arts are in the Appendix. Another useful source on this subject is *The Conflict Management Skills Workshop: a trainer's guide*, Withers (2002). This is a comprehensive facilitator's handbook which provides outlines for workshops of different duration, with suggested activities, sample flipcharts, and trainer's tips.

The role of counselling, already described in Chapter 4 and referred to earlier in this chapter, is an important part of management. The manager's behaviour should encourage staff to seek advice when required, but at the same time ensure that management style does not prevent the individual taking initiatives. The delegation process requires all participants to be clear about the amount of responsibility that is being delegated, and in what circumstances decisions need to be referred back to the manager. Mutual trust and confidence, vital to teamwork, are most likely to emerge where there are clear guidelines on responsibility. Having responsibility for a particular task, even for a short time, makes the individual think about all aspects of that task and can result in suggestions for possible streamlining of the methods and systems in operation. If job rotation is to be effective each period of responsibility needs to be long enough for this to happen, but not so long that the individual eventually loses interest, seeing the task not as a challenge but rather as an obstacle to progress. This is where a detailed individual staff file, already mentioned as being fundamental to appraisal and counselling interviews, can be a useful management tool. Details of work schedules and time-recording will help in planning an individual's progress as well as in overall staff-planning. In organisations where all staff are required to record their time for charging purposes, e.g. accounting firms and legal practices, copies of completed time records will provide a valuable breakdown of time spent on particular types of work and indicate future staffing needs, and the way in which the information service could best be directed. This in turn will help in overall resource-planning and budgeting.

If you are interested in finding out more about management, you could consider membership of the UK's Chartered Management Institute or the relevant body in your country of operation. Most will have lists of courses and conferences as well as other management activities. A comprehensive listing of executive courses and initiatives in Europe can be found in the *European directory on executive education*, EFMD (2000). The act of managing a service opens up a whole range of opportunities for job enhancement, personal growth and career development, not just for the manager, but for everyone involved in the provision of that service. One way of making a service function exciting is to actively develop your products and skills and to market them, adopting a marketplace philosophy. This puts the service in a stronger position to contend with others for budgets, approval for projects, and other resources. Thus the effective manager helps to ensure the service's future development, as demonstrated by the following real-life example.

Case study 2

Melanie Goody, now Director of Web Services in KPMG's UK Marketing, Knowledge & Communications Group, provides an excellent example of the way in which developing management skills as well as technical knowledge can lead to career progression and success.

Melanie's interest in information work and IT applications began when she joined the Halifax Building Society as a clerk/cashier during her 'gap' year. She was subsequently promoted to head of the investment department at the branch, which proved to be extremely timely in that that was the year in which the Halifax introduced computerised systems. Melanie was given responsibility for IT training and troubleshooting for the branch and as a result decided to study librarianship and information science full time.

Following study at what was then Ealing College of Higher Education in London (now part of Thames Valley University) and achieving top marks in her professional examinations, she took her first post as Librarian with a chemical engineering firm, where she stayed for three years.

Those years opened up the world of industry and commerce providing a useful learning situation and the opportunity to carry out a whole range of activities, ranging from the provision of information and research services to the production of a current awareness (abstracting) bulletin, in addition to organising acquisition and subscription services and carrying out cataloguing and indexing. An exciting additional opportunity came with the invitation to spend six weeks on secondment as the librarian at the company's Netherlands office in the Hague, managing the library in the absence of the head of the service.

This period provided a sound base from which to make the next career move and in 1982 Melanie joined Peat Marwick Mitchell & Co, a major UK accounting firm, subsequently renamed Peat Marwick, as Library Manager of their Technical Advisory Department. Again information technology offered considerable scope for personal development with responsibilities that included the introduction of electronic information sources and the development of automated library management and purchasing systems.

In 1987 changes in the firm's structure proved to be the start of a long term opportunity for career development. Peat Marwick merged with KMG Thomson McLintock to become KPMG Thomson McLintock and Melanie was appointed Head of Research and Information Services. As such she was responsible for the amalgamation of the two firms' libraries and the development of an information service and subsequently managed the merger of all of the management consultancy and accounting libraries and the development of a UK-wide Research and Information service.

Melanie found that with all the change occurring within the firm she certainly did not need to look elsewhere for personal development. In 1987 she began working as a management consultant within KPMG's public sector consulting practice acting initially as a specialist consultant on projects related to libraries and information services, including market tests of four central government libraries. Her involvement in client service work increased rapidly and in 1996 she was seconded on a full-time basis as an Executive Consultant in the Development Initiatives Group. Her role within the group included acting as lead consultant and Engagement Manager on a number of projects, including strategy reviews, Lottery bids and Private Finance Initiative (PFI) engagements.

In October 1997 Melanie joined KPMG's UK Knowledge Management Group as Head of Information Development. This brought with it responsibility for co-ordinating the UK firm's purchases of external information, and for the development and integration of external content on the firm's intranet. The Knowledge Management Group sponsors the desktop delivery of external information to all KPMG's UK staff; this information includes newsfeeds, company information, historical press comment and technical and legal reference materials. She has also represented the UK firm in various projects relating to the development of KPMG's global intranet, including the selection of global content providers since 1998.

In 1999 Melanie became the Head of KM Operations, UK Knowledge Management Group (UK KMG) and her responsibilities increased to include all the services which the UK KMG provided to KPMG. These included the UK intranet, market research, the business information service, external content acquisition, the client database, and the contacts database. Responsibility for the CVs database also fell within her remit. This was developed as an internal global database allowing quick identification of those with particular expertise and experience within KPMG. Melanie's role then expanded further to include the development of protocols and standards for intranet sites and the implementation of best practices in the design and development of intranet sites. This was followed in 2000 by promotion to the post of Director of KM Operations in which she represented the Europe, Middle East & Africa region (EMA) in international discussions relating to global content acquisition and management. KPMG projects in that role included the identification of global newsfeed requirements and the development of a functional specification for potential newsfeed providers. In January 2003 she was appointed to her present role, which she sees as offering further exciting opportunities.

Melanie also sees it as important to contribute to and learn from professional involvement outside the firm. She has been a member of the Library

Association (LA)'s Accreditation Board, the Council of the Institute of Information Scientists (IIS) and the IIS Professional Standards and Development Committee. [In April 2002 the LA and the IIS merged to form the Chartered Institute of Information Professionals (CILIP)]. She is a founder member and former Chairman of the City Information Group and former Chair of the Coalition for Public Information (CoPI).

Equally important is always to be ready to learn more, at all stages of your career. Melanie has attended numerous courses and is grateful for KPMG's excellent training and development programme, mentioning some of the internal courses as being particularly good, for example, Presentation Skills, European Management Consulting, and the firm's Senior Manager Development Workshop. Among external courses she found that one on Making a Business Case has stood her in good stead in achieving a number of objectives, not least in presenting budget proposals. She emphasises the importance of keeping up with the professional press in order to spot trends and identify emerging issues.

The above case study illustrates the wide range of areas of management through which you can successfully pursue a career, by building on earlier experience, adding new skills, and opening new paths to explore. Ideas for further development are discussed in the final chapter.

References

Barker, Alan (2002)
How to manage meetings. London: Kogan Page

Blackwell, Edward (2002)
How to prepare a business plan. London: Kogan Page

Brookson, Stephen (2000)
Managing budgets. London: Dorling Kindersley

Brown, Mark (2002)
Project management in a week. London: Hodder & Stoughton

Business Information Testdrive. Monthly journal, Headland Business Information

Charney, Cy & Conway, Kathy (1997)
The Trainer's Toolkit. New York: AMACOM

Corrall, Sheila (2000)
Strategic management of information services: a planning handbook. London: Aslib

European Foundation for Management Development (2000)
European directory on executive education. Brussels: EFMD

Fisher, Kimball (2000)
Leading self-directed work teams. New expanded edition. New York: McGraw-Hill

Gabay, J. Jonathan (2002)
Web marketing in a week. 2nd edition. London: Hodder & Stoughton

Haynes, Marion E. (2000)
Making every minute count. 3rd edition. London: Kogan Page

Jay, Ros (2001)
Fast thinking: presentation. London: Pearson Education

Leigh, Andrew & Maynard, Michael (2002)
Leading your team: how to involve and inspire teams. 2nd edition. London: Nicholas Brealey

Maitland, Iain (2002)
Business plans in a week. 3rd edition. London: Hodder & Stoughton

Rowntree, Derek (2000)
The manager's book of checklists. London: Pearson Education /Prentice Hall

Video Arts
Dealing with conflict (training video)

Video Arts
Not my type: valuing diversity (training video + supporting training material)

Webb, Sylvia P. (1996)
Creating an information service. 3rd edition London: Aslib

Withers, Bill (2002)
The Conflict Management Skills Workshop: a trainer's guide. New York: AMACOM

Chapter 6

Advancing through information

Information is vital to everyone's job, but for the information professional it is of paramount importance because it is the commodity in which he or she deals. What an exciting commodity with which to be associated; constant change takes place not only in its content and the amount that is available, but also in its format and the ways in which it can be organised and exploited. With the rise of Knowledge Management, and the increasing emphasis, within many private and public sector bodies, on developing as a 'learning organisation' there are ever increasing development opportunities within the workplace for the proactive information professional.

The choice is wide, and you must decide what is possible and appropriate in the light of your particular work situation, both in terms of the needs of the department and wider organisational activities. So which broad areas of information and knowledge provision and use could be seen to offer means of enhancement, both for the service and those who provide it?

Organisation and arrangement of information

If information is to be a widely available resource, it must be organised so that it is easily accessible physically and without too many imposed restraints, such as restricted hours or cumbersome procedures and limitations on use. As well as being readily available, information must be arranged so that it is recognisably easy to use. So the organisation and arrangement of information offers one area in which, through seeking improvements for users, the information worker can experience personal development. Where should you start?

The organisation and arrangement of information falls under two broad headings: physical location and logical sequence. Organising and arranging resources requires the use of various procedures for grouping and listing. So why not start by noting specific considerations under some general headings as shown in the following examples? From these you can identify those to which it would be both appropriate and interesting to give special attention. Perhaps you believe that your reference collection is not being used as much as it ought to be, or that there are problems with filing and finding press cuttings, reports or non-print media. No doubt you can add other examples which relate to the particular service that you give.

Example 1

PHYSICAL ARRANGEMENT
(always to be thought of with the user in mind)

- ease of access
- central location of the information unit as a whole
- overall attractiveness to users
- ease of locating the most-used items
- clear labelling
- display of simple instructions beside equipment
- provision of well-designed work areas, with study tables, chairs, etc.
- storage and arrangement of non-book material.

Example 2

LOGICAL ARRANGEMENT

- by subject e.g. formally classified or by key word
- by format e.g. paper copies of company reports and records in alphabetical sequence by company name or by business activity; dictionaries by language; maps and atlases by country; CDs of newspapers and journals by title then date; diskettes according to coverage; journals by title, then date; books; videos
- related procedures e.g. classification, cataloguing, indexing.

You will need to make the same considerations for hardcopy or when building a database. Your priority is to develop a logical sequence to allow straightforward retrieval, whatever format the information is in. The simple act of drawing up such lists will help you decide on any particular aspects which require special attention and at the same time may be relevant to your personal development plan, or that of anyone else in the department. For instance, in Example 2, you may feel that it is necessary to reclassify. This will require you to look at existing schemes and review current practice among colleagues, backed up by further reading and perhaps an updating course. First you should ask the question, does the present scheme merit expansion, or is reclassification required? To answer it you will need to draw up a list of the criteria to be met by a classification scheme. The checklist below, revised slightly from its original in Webb (1996a), will help.

CHECKLIST: SELECTING A CLASSIFICATION SCHEME

1. Does it cover all the subject areas envisaged as being included in the LIS over the next five years?

2. Does it cater for general works as well as specialist subjects?

3. Is it up-to-date and capable of expansion/ modification?

4. Is there a good index to the scheme, e.g. is it detailed, does it give cross references to preferred and related terms?

5. Is it easy to use, e.g. does it have a single notation, i.e. letters or numbers; can the codes be kept short; are the sequences logical and easy to follow?

6. Could it be used equally well electronically for database building as well as online cataloguing?

7. Has it proved useful in libraries with similar needs?

8. Which sections were found most appropriate in other centres if the scheme was not used in full?

9. Had any other scheme previously been in use in these centres?

10. What do they see as the main advantages and disadvantages of the present scheme?

11. What modifications have been made by other libraries and information centres?

You also need to ask how much additional staff effort would be required and, above all, what are the real benefits to the users?

These are just some of the questions requiring answers, which will help you in your decision-making process. It must be emphasised that these questions and considerations are just examples and may not include everything that you might need to cover for your particular set-up.Their purpose is to open up new ways of looking at the service, and by doing so to provide a means of identifying potential areas of staff development.

Moving into Knowledge Management

If you are working within an organisation where Knowledge Management is already established, your role may well include some responsibility for managing or codifying its internal knowledge assets. You may for example have responsibility for web content development, be building products for the company's intranet, or be managing a knowledge 'hub' of other information workers within a formal knowledge network infrastructure. What more you can do will clearly depend on your individual situation, but here are some questions to ask yourself:

- Is knowledge being captured and managed in the most appropriate way for the organisation's business objectives?

- Are there knowledge initiatives which were launched with a great fanfare but which in fact have failed to deliver the promised benefits?

- Are there opportunities to propose, project-manage or coordinate new knowledge-related initiatives?

- Are your own skills and expertise being used to optimum effect?

- Could you be more effective in this area with a skills upgrade?

You may not be sure what skills and competencies are actually required. As Webb (1998) points out, business awareness and the ability to work with others are equally as important as research and analysis skills. For anyone working in the field of information and knowledge management, a range of skills will be required. Whether you are already working in a Knowledge Management capacity, or are hoping to do so, you may find it useful to assess your own skills levels in general day-to-day operational skills and knowledge and information management skills from the table opposite — reproduced from Webb (1988).

If you are a relative novice in this area, perhaps with an interest in knowledge management and some training in it as part of a professional qualification, but working in an organisation which has not yet taken it fully on board, where do you start? Skyrme (1999) offers some very practical suggestions on action planning for the information professional wishing to develop as the 'knowledgeable' interface between the user and repositories of information. An essential part of this will be to identify and develop closer partnerships with knowledge champions in your own organisation – the people who can make things happen. Skyrme is also insistent that you should apply some of the core knowledge management practices to yourself and your unit: "What do you really know about your customers, business processes and people? Are you continuing to learn and improve your service? Have you valued your own and your library's 'intellectual capital'? Have you sought out best practice, wherever it is? When did you last benchmark your activities against a comparable activity externally?" You can usefully start with some practical 'quick wins' that will provide early (and visible) benefits. These could include:

- a knowledge inventory i.e. a database of internal expertise

- contact database of external expertise

- databases of good practice and precedents

- templates of standard documents that are regularly used.

If another part of the organisation is developing an interesting new project, why not propose yourself as its information coordinator? The higher your profile is within the organisation, the better chance you will have of

General day-to-day operational skills

- **understanding of the organisation's**
  - business & activities
- **computer applications**
  - word processing
  - graphics
  - spreadsheets
  - CD-ROMs
  - online/networks/e-mail
- **interpersonal skills**
- **oral communication**
- **written communication**
  - appropriate style
  - presentation
- **personal work management**
  - use of time
  - assigning priorities
  - recording results
  - meeting deadlines
- **management**
  - planning
  - decision making
  - human resources
  - finance
- **organisation involvement**

Knowledge & information management skills

- **knowledge of sources**
  - print/electronic
  - internal/external
  - who to ask
  - how to look
  - evaluation
- **subject knowledge & understanding**
- **information & records management**
  - indexing methods
  - database development
  - thesaurus construction
  - retrieval/delivery methods
  - electronic storage
  - retention policy
  - structuring records
  - legislation, standards & controls
- **networks (internal/external)**
- **users/patterns of usage**
  - needs analysis
  - satisfaction measures
- **current awareness services**
  - monitoring/updating
  - abstracting
  - news services e.g. via bulletins, Websites
- **user advice & training**
- **contribution to knowledge & information strategy**

being recognised as an informed professional with something valuable to offer. Make sure that you keep up to date with current issues in knowledge management, by reading, attending seminars and briefings, and subscribing to e-mailed newsletters such as the Gurteen Knowledge-Letter and KnowledgeBoard.

Case study 3

Michael Everson, Knowledge Manager at **ttsp**, the renowned architectural and interior design practice, is proof of the transformation that can be effected by the implementation of Knowledge Management into a conventional library framework. Michael joined the company 6 years ago. At that time, "the original job description was for a traditional corporate librarian with specialised subject knowledge and experience in the architectural/construction sector. I had the requisite experience, having worked in the sector for ten years after qualifying as a librarian – I also had the desire to design and implement a Knowledge Management strategy within a corporate environment. I already had a great interest in this emerging concept and having researched the topic and attended one or two courses and seminars, I followed its progress and development with avid interest. I tried to transmit my enthusiasm and understanding of the benefits of Knowledge Management to my then employer, a long established multi-disciplinary architectural practice, then undergoing major change at every level, including Chief Executive. Sadly they were reluctant to try this new approach, even though the time was just right for them.

When I saw the post of librarian advertised by **ttsp**, I already knew the company by reputation and my subsequent research confirmed they were a forward-thinking company, with major changes about to take place at senior level. I applied for the post and in due course attended the first interview. At my instigation, the discussion came round to the concept of Knowledge Management, something the Chief Executive had heard about before but did not understand as a concept. Then and at the subsequent second interview, we talked more about Knowledge Management and when I was offered the post it was on the understanding that my new employer would give me the opportunity to analyse the company and put forward a Knowledge Management strategy to best suit the business.

I have omitted to say that at the first interview it struck me that I was denied the opportunity of seeing the library – at the second interview I understood why!

The Library Information Centre I inherited had been in existence for many years, operating well under a number of different librarians. It was entirely a 'hard copy' environment that had been most recently badly neglected. Absolutely every flat surface had literature of every description randomly piled up to a depth of two feet, nothing on these surfaces catalogued or documented in any way. Journals had been literally thrown into cupboards unsorted and of the shelf stock, nothing had been withdrawn or culled for a very long time. The primary book stock, including legislation and very important standards, were all held in closed and locked, waist-high tambour fronted cabinets – hardly conducive to an open, knowledge-sharing working environment! I was very aware that the interviewers watched my reactions very closely!

A daunting scenario but strangely enough apt for what was about to happen. I accepted the challenge and knowing that during the interim period of a month before I could start the situation would get worse, I made a mental note to bring a camera with me on my first day in the new job! This I did and in those early days of dust, culling, more dust, database design and cataloguing, even more dust and skip filling (four very full skip-loads in total) when my spirits were low, I could look back on those first images and see proof of the progress being made.

During this time it was imperative that I got to know some very important facts; namely the current perception of 'information' in the company; whether it was used to best advantage; who the key information gate-keepers were and, perhaps more importantly develop rapport with staff at all levels and build their trust in the Library Information Centre and its staff – at that point comprising only me.

The first twelve months were crucial – my learning curve, the analysis of the company and trust building - so that when the time came to make recommendations for a radical change in strategy and investment in the unit (that was eventually to become the Knowledge Centre) the staff at all levels would know I had their best interests at heart."

Michael agrees with the general view that a successful knowledge management strategy must be led from the top, so it is vital that the Board or Partners, whatever the nomenclature of the decision makers, are fully on-board with the concept. If there is dissent on the subject at senior level the KM programme at best will be flawed, at worst will just not get off the ground. This process can be very demanding, and success will not happen overnight. Michael continues:

"To implement the KM programme I designed at **ttsp** demanded a great deal of individual lobbying, discussions and presentations at Board level intensively over a six-month period, culminating in a final, make-or-break, full-board presentation, the KM topic being the primary subject booked for discussion that day. When the go-ahead was unanimously given the feeling was shock more than anything else!

Since then, the KM journey at **ttsp** has taken on great impetus, at times running off at tangents but always coming back on track for mainstream implementation. The KM team (for part of the strategy agreed was to provide additional staff – proof that the Board buy-in was genuine, putting their money where their mouths were!) have developed a whole new respect for information and knowledge company-wide. We have developed a new Knowledge Management technology 'vehicle'; custom-designed for the needs of the practice and we are currently using this to encourage the concept of sharing knowledge within the practice – historically anathema in the sector as a whole."

Michael believes that the process of getting a KM strategy adopted has been invaluable for his own personal development, saying, "It was extremely important that I developed a high profile within the organisation, engendering trust and showing that I fully understood the working patterns of the different studios and divisions. I truly had to raise my head 'above the parapet', to demonstrate I could work at director level as well as with the new student input each year. I had to hone and develop the presentation skills I had already acquired *en route*, to be sure that the KM message when delivered, was not watered down by poor personal skills. I had to be prepared to stand my ground when challenged, to ensure that I fully understood the implications of what I was asking from the staff. Although not a naturally shy person, I had to be very sure that I believed absolutely in the concept I was so ardently propounding, to enable me to do the concept justice.

I had to change my own perceptions. The attributes required by a Knowledge Manager are different to the traditional 'service' role attributes of the librarian – a pro-active approach is vital from start to finish, in every way. In the fullness of time, because of the approach I took with the introduction of KM, the directors saw that I was capable of not just delivering the message internally but helping them win projects by joining presentation teams to bid for new work. They encouraged me to spread the word about the concept of Knowledge Management and show how it enhanced the efficiency of the practice and that there was the knock-on benefit to their clients. The Chief Executive commented recently that the **ttsp** Knowledge Centre had received more press coverage in the sector journals than had our projects!

My career has developed rapidly, thanks to embracing this new corporate philosophy wholeheartedly and I have been invited to give seminars and lectures on the subject in the UK, the rest of Europe and the United States since word of the Knowledge Centre has circulated. I have been interviewed a number of times and asked to write articles in the architectural press. Because of the international nature of the sector I work in and the research element so vital in pro-active KM, I am fortunate enough to travel worldwide on behalf of the practice, always sharing my findings and knowledge with the company when I return - the essence of KM is sharing! My work thrills me – no job or company is perfect – but I truly enjoy what I do, though there are never enough hours in the day!"

Sources of information

The next broad area to look at is that of sources of information. Sources will comprise items of a general nature common to most collections, e.g. basic general reference tools; and those which are subject-specific and therefore not as widely available. The format will vary, as will the time-span covered and regularity of updating. The amount of detail given, and the authoritative nature of sources, are other aspects to consider, not forgetting the scarcity value and confidentiality of certain information.

How is personal development possible in this area? First through carrying out a thorough review of your own resources. However familiar you may be with your stock, you will still uncover some items whose full potential you had not completely realised. Others you will reassess in the light of past usefulness, bearing in mind any changes which may have occurred in the organisation's information needs. Format must also be reconsidered, e.g. by considering the following questions.

- Are services previously available only in hard copy now available in other formats, and would any of them be more appropriate in terms of space-saving, time-saving, cost?

- How frequently would a different format be used?

- How convenient would it be for your users?

- Is suitable equipment already available in-house?

- What is available in other departments i.e. the organisation's total information resource?

- How would any resultant change affect your budget?

The relevance of coverage according to the time-span of the information is another consideration. It is as important to discard material or delete records which are no longer required as it is to add new items.

When looking at the sources of information that you have, ask yourself whether better use could be made of them, perhaps by publicising them more widely and in new ways, or whether they could be grouped for more effective subject searching. For example, one useful way of grouping web resources is to set up themed folders contained bookmarks of relevant sites, which are regularly scanned and updated, providing your users with a ready-made collection of sites of interest to them.

In considering how to make the best use of your own sources of information, you will also identify gaps in coverage. The next step is to contemplate how best to cope with those gaps. Should they be filled by further acquisition? If so, will this be in electronic or print format? If print, this need not necessarily be by purchase but could be through exchange with other centres, from the various 'offers' lists often seen in the professional journals. Reciprocal arrangements with other libraries may include exchange of in-house publications; access to each other's stock on a reference basis; mutually convenient exchange of information and advice by telephone, fax or e-mail; occasional loans and the provision of photocopies and perhaps print-outs (although it may be necessary to charge for these). Personal contacts are a very valuable part of information work and can certainly enrich the store of information available to both parties. It is worth noting that books no longer relevant to your needs could be useful to librarians in other countries. Book Aid International (formerly the Ranfurly Library Service) can advise on this (see Appendix).

Contact with and use of external resources offers considerable scope for individual development. The seeking and finding of appropriate external sources of information requires initiative. That in itself is satisfying, particularly where you are unable to use the most obvious source for reasons of confidentiality. It can further result in an increased awareness of the existence of many specialist associations, and access to the range of services which they may provide, and lead to an increase in your knowledge of subjects hitherto unexplored.

Format

In looking at sources you cannot help but be aware of the format in which the information is presented. Working with non-book material which requires specialist handling, e.g. film and video, cassettes, slides, maps, photographs and archival collections, can open up a whole new series of possibilities for those who may previously have worked only with hard-copy resources.

The commercial potential of information in its increasingly varied formats also suggests areas for self-development. Databases originally designed to meet in-house needs could be reconsidered as commercial products. The growth of web technology, with its range of applications, has resulted in whole new ways of thinking about information. In addition to the computer's standard capacity for streamlining administrative tasks, its ability to list, cross-reference and store material from a variety of sources, has enabled information to be far more quickly identified, accessed and exploited.

As well as the obvious benefits to the information retrieval process, and the increased opportunity to maximise the exploration of information resources, technology now plays a pervasive role in library housekeeping, with tasks such as circulation control, cataloguing and book ordering routinely automated, regardless of the size of the library or library management system. These can offer possibilities for improvement of services, and also make possible the kind of collaboration and inter-library networking that a few years ago would only have been feasible for the very largest libraries. The development of electronic community information services, the growth of electronic resource development at a national level, and the increasing popularity of large-scale digitisation projects (such as those funded in the UK by the New Opportunities Fund and the Heritage Lotteries Fund) offer exciting developmental opportunities in terms of technical skills upgrading, content selection and management, regional or national cooperation and partnership working with organisations in a range of sectors.

The growth of information (and the finding aids to it) in electronic format have highlighted the need for effective ICT (Information and Communications Technology) training of information staff, a need high-lighted in reports such as the one by the Library and Information Commission (1998) which built on a training needs analysis conducted by BECTa, the British Educational Communications and Technology agency. The implementation nationwide of the People's Network in UK public libraries has given a massive boost to staff training, with the widespread adoption of the European Computer Driving Licence as the basic level of competence that all staff should attain. Large-scale initiatives such as the People's Network have not just raised the question of staff training, but also the role of information staff in training users to make the most of the new opportunities now on offer. How can they best help users to help themselves in terms of finding relevant information and evaluating its usefulness? Even within quite small organisations, improving 'informa-tion literacy' is becoming increasingly vital as a tool to combat perceived information overload and improve the quality of decision-making, and who is better qualified to lead on this than an information professional? By providing practical guidance, through structured group sessions in the information centre or one-to-one discussions at the desk-top, there is a real opportunity here both to make a measurable contribution to the organisa-tion and to underline your own professionalism and usefulness.

Considerations regarding the use of the data that can be collected about individuals have been brought to the fore in the UK with the introduction of the Data Protection Act 1998 and the Freedom of Information Act 2000. These have in themselves provided a personal development opportunity for some information staff, who have adopted an additional role as the Data Controller or the central point for advice and information for their organisations on the implications of the Acts for them (the Information Commissioner's web site provides detailed guidance on both Acts). The growing importance of electronic copyright law offers another opening.

Online searching skills have always been highly valued, and a good knowledge of the rapidly increasing number of information sources which are available electronically, and how to use them, can enhance the status of information staff in the eyes of others, adding a new dimension to their perceived role, ability, and knowledge. One often-forgotten aspect of this is the acquisition of keyboard skills. The more hours a day you spend online or using a computer for administrative tasks, the more essential a course in keyboard skills becomes if you are to make the most effective use of time and minimise the physical strain of poor posture and fingering. Even if your keyboard technique is fine, you may still feel that you would benefit from a short course to improve some aspect of IT, or to update your knowledge of information sources in a particular area. When selecting a course, pick one that has been designed with the needs of the librarian or information officer in mind, and one that suits your particular requirements. Aslib, for example, runs a series of courses on different types of information available online, e.g. Business Information on the Internet and more technical courses such as Knowledgeware on Trial. Cimtech, mentioned in the previous chapter, is the UK's centre of expertise on all aspects of information management and technology. Cimtech offers consultancy, short courses and seminars, and publications, including a bi-monthly journal *Information Media & Technology* which contains detailed evaluations of products, as well as articles on how specific companies use particular products. Cimtech's address is in the Appendix. Keep seeking improvement by consulting others, e.g. experienced users, professional associations; joining a user group; keeping yourself up to date by reading the relevant journals and newsletters; and taking advantage of any seminars organised by software houses and database producers.

Enquiry work

Whatever sources of information you use, in whatever format, they must hold the answers to the enquiries that you receive, and be the basis of any special services that you provide, e.g. personalised SDI (selective dissemination of information), newsletters, bulletins, research, training, all of which in themselves offer scope for personal development in information needs analysis, communication skills, and research techniques, including the art of scanning the literature. The enquiry is likely to be the central feature of much information work and as such must be handled skilfully and efficiently to ensure the highest quality of response to the enquirer's request. How does such a response come about? By understanding exactly what is required, and by finding the information and presenting it in precise, easy-to-read form. What means can be used to achieve this satisfactory outcome? The answer is the well-organised 'reference interview' or 'information interview', the working-out and use of which will help develop your own logical thinking processes and communication skills, as well as improve librarian/user relationships.

Enquiries may be made face-to-face, by telephone, or via written correspondence, fax, e-mail or in web form. They may be made by the person requiring the information, or by his or her representative. Some form of reference interview is required for all but the simplest request, and dictates the strategy for your search, no matter which sources of information you eventually consult. You can draw up a flowchart either on paper or on your computer screen to take you through the stages of the interview. It could be incorporated into the enquiry form on which the steps and outcome of the search will also be recorded. It is not necessary to record everything that the enquirer says - establish what is required and put it into a clear, concise form ready for the necessary research.

The initial question may differ greatly from what is actually required, therefore it helps the searcher to know the purpose of the request. As Hoskisson (1997) points out, "effective reference service is only possible when the real question has been asked and understood". As well as establishing exactly what is required, with details of time-span and depth of coverage, you must always ask what the deadline is. It is no good carrying out a comprehensive search if the information arrives too late for the enquirer's purpose. There is a good deal of guidance in the published literature. Bates (1999) counsels "Keep as a mantra: the client has the best understanding of what information is needed; I have the best understanding of where the information is". Peterson (1997) provides a review of various models of question negotiation in what is a very complex human interaction.

A relatively new and exciting area of development is the 'virtual reference interview', as reference librarians use the web for their work, creating web pages to provide answers to anticipated reference questions or frequently asked questions (FAQs), and to help themselves organise and locate information. Two such services are described by Viles (1999) whose article also gives details of Robert Travica's 'five characteristics of the virtual library' and proposes some virtual equivalences of non-verbal behaviour such as eye contact and tone of voice.

Promoting the service

Having established a comprehensive information service, with enthusiastic, personable and efficient staff, you will want to ensure that it is used. A service is only of use to those who know about it and appreciate its full potential. You must work out the best means of promoting your particular service; different approaches will be appropriate in different organisations. In addition to your web site, tours, formal presentations backed up by colourful visual aids, newsletters and guides are just some of the other ways in which this can be achieved, and will bring into play the interpersonal and communication skills described in the previous chapter. Face-to-face presentations are perhaps the most effective means of promoting your service as they allow you to project enthusiasm as well as professionalism, and of course to answer questions and demonstrate the overall helpful and knowledgeable nature of the LIS and its staff. Making a presentation gives you the chance to combine the use of management and information skills. Aslib's one-day Presentation Skills course gives participants practical opportunities to prepare and deliver presentations in a supportive environment under the guidance of the tutor. These presentations are video-recorded and reviewed constructively by the presenter, the tutor and the other delegates. You will also learn a lot from watching other people and deciding what does or does not appeal to you in their presentations. CILIP's Publicity and Public Relations Group, which exists to demonstrate to the library and information profession that continuous and planned public relations practice is essential in every type of library, organises day courses and conferences, with themes including graphic design and print, copy writing, public relations and marketing. The Group has produced a range of publications covering public relations, leaflet design, copy-writing and working with the media. Other suggestions are to be found in Coote and Batchelor (1998). Such activities can have very valuable spin-off in terms of staff motivation. By being asked to be involved, everyone in the department will feel that their contribution is valued. Brainstorming sessions can open up a whole new way of looking at things, as well as achieving job satisfaction, and can be used equally successfully for management or information-related development.

An example of this approach is the way in which a guide to a Business Information Service in its early days was put together at Stoy Hayward (now BDO Stoy Hayward). It had already been decided that, as the service had been significantly changed and developed over the previous two years, a guide was needed. This would be aimed at all members of the firm from new trainee accountants to partners. It would indicate the scope of the service in an easy-to-follow, easy-to-use format, avoiding jargon, i.e. written from the user's viewpoint. An alphabetical arrangement was thought to be the most appropriate form for this, so avoiding the need for an index, yet offering quick reference. A meeting of LIS staff for the pooling of ideas resulted in decisions on what to cover, and who would write which sections. It was decided to include subject areas, sources, and types of information in one sequence, with a brief one-page introduction on the objectives of the service, and a further page giving details of the information staff available to help users. A list of journal holdings was also thought to be useful, and was incorporated as an appendix. The next step was to list each entry to be included. The work was divided according to interest and specialism. For example, the member of staff who had a special interest in the organisation of accounting and auditing standards took responsibility for those subjects, as well as covering other more general headings. In order to ensure consistency, the overall editing was carried out by one person, who checked that relevant *see* and *see also* references were included where necessary. With documents such as this created and stored electronically, updating is a simple matter (but do remember to withdraw out of date print and electronic versions from circulation).

As an exercise in teamwork it was very rewarding, giving everyone a chance to use their professional and specialist interest skills, to feel that their contribution was valuable, and above all to work together on a task which would result in a product for which they could each take credit. This type of joint activity gives the manager further insights into each individual's abilities, potential, and degree of job satisfaction, and can provide a natural juncture at which to switch responsibilities around.

Continuing Education

Another method of information-related development - one which can co-ordinate several of the areas mentioned and which certainly has positive benefits for the service - is to pursue a further course of study in an information area. A number of universities and colleges now offer these on a part-time basis, so that there need be no career break. These range from the City & Guild's and the Scottish Qualifications Authority's (SQA) modules, to diplomas and higher degrees, and increasingly require no college attendance, being available through distance or open learning programmes. Among the pioneers in open learning in the library and information field, Edinburgh's Telford College has students from all over the world. The college has also developed courses for those who whilst holding qualifications in other fields, would like to acquire library and information skills. For example teachers and others can now pursue a Telford course on 'Running a School Library', and there are others on library technology and staff supervision, all available by open learning. The various part-time master's degrees on offer include for example the City University's MSc in Information Science and MA in Arts Management. The Department of Information Studies, University College of Wales, Aberystwyth offers a number of distance-learning programmes at undergraduate and postgraduate level in the management of library and information services. CILIP provides details on its web site (under Careers and Qualifications) of a list of accredited courses, entitled *Where to study in the UK*. International students wishing to study in the UK may be eligible for funding via the British Council. Go to the Council's website at *www.britishcouncil.org* and select 'education' for details of scholarships and other funding.

Case study 4

Michael Oberwarth works for a large law firm in London. Starting as a temporary Information Clerk, he progressed to a full time position in the company as Information Officer as a direct result of undertaking an MA course in Information Services Management at the University of North London (UNL; now part of London Metropolitan University). Michael did some shopping around before deciding where he wanted to go: "One library school I looked at was very focused on the old, traditional skills. UNL seemed more modern; it had courses on things like intranet design and academic libraries and health, which focused on particular areas. I recommend to other library trainees that they go to UNL".

Michael himself did the module option on managing an intranet/extranet project, which gave him a good mix of theory and practical design skills, which he hopes to use in the workplace. As with other elements of the course, Michael selected options that combined his genuine interest in the subject with topics that offered potential benefits to his company. For example, he was keen to explore the question of legal research training within private law firms. As he says, "in an industry where information is required quickly, it is important that people know where to look for answers to questions, whether it be on databases on in books. When they arrive at law firms, many trainees don't have the basic skills necessary to research even simple queries". Michael's research into the content and scope of legal research training on offer to trainee solicitors and Legal Practices Course students has raised some interesting questions about the information expectations that law firms and legal departments have about the legal research skills of their trainees and students, and how far their courses reflect this. This has obvious practical value for his own employers.

Of course it isn't easy. Getting back into the habit of carrying out research, studying and writing essays, while trying to balance academic and work responsibilities, and quite often family ones as well, is very challenging. Michael's approach: choosing a course that he really wanted to do, that would also provide potential business benefits is a good way of maintaining motivation and impetus – as well as identifying new career opportunities.

Such courses can make you look at yourself and your organisation with a fresh eye. That is just what you have to do - remain constantly aware of everything around you. Otherwise you may overlook possible changes which could improve the service, and miss opportunities for the further development of yourself and your staff.

Printed References

Bates, Mary Ellen (1999)
"What do you really want to know? The reference interview." *One-Person Library* 15 (9), pp. 1-3

Business Information Service: a guide. 3rd edition. London: Stoy Hayward, 1990

Coote, Helen and Batchelor, Bridget (1998)
How to market your library service effectively. 2nd edition. London: Aslib

Data Protection Act 1998. Norwich: The Stationery Office

Freedom of Information Act 2000. Norwich: The Stationery Office

Hoskisson, Tam (1997)
"Making the right assumptions: know your user and improve the reference interview." *Reference Librarian* no. 59, pp. 67-75

Library and Information Commission (1998)
Building the new library network. London: Library and Information Commission

Peterson, Lisa C (1997)
"Effective question negotiation in the reference interview." *Current Studies in Librarianship* 21(1/2), pp. 22-34

Skyrme, David (1999)
"Knowledge Management: making it work." *Law Librarian* 30 (2), pp. 84-90

Viles, Ann (1999)
"The virtual reference interview: equivalencies. A discussion proposal." Iflanet Discussion Group on Reference Work Report, www.ifla.org/VII/dg/dgrw/dp99-06.htm

Webb, Sylvia P. (1996a)
Creating an information service. 3rd edition. London: Aslib

Webb, Sylvia P. (1998)
Knowledge Management: linchpin of change. London: Aslib

Website References

Gurteen Knowledge-Letter. Available from: mailto:knowledge-letter@gurteen.com

Information Commissioner, www.dataprotection.gov.uk/

KnowledgeBoard. Available from: subscribe@knowledgeboard.com

Chapter 7

On your Own

Many people are attracted by the idea of becoming an independent consultant, often without thinking too hard about what it is, or what it would involve. Perhaps they have been in the same job for a long time, and feel in a bit of a rut, or they may have been made redundant and are looking to fill in time and make some money until a 'real' job comes along. On cold winter mornings, the idea of a cosy home office can be very appealing! With information and knowledge management higher on political and organisational agendas than they have ever been, there are certainly tremendous opportunities for the skilled information professional – but you do need to be very clear about what you can offer as a consultant, and what the implications (financial and otherwise) are of going it alone.

What do consultants actually do?

But what do they actually do? The word 'consultant' is used a lot: think of 'beauty consultant' and 'recruitment consultant' for example. A working definition of a consultant for the purposes of this chapter might be:

An independent and experienced professional who provides advice or guidance to organisations planning or undergoing a process of structured change.

Just to highlight three elements: independent (i.e. not tied to potential suppliers of goods or services e.g. particular software vendors); there is an element of advice, which we will look at more closely below; and there is always an element of change, and managing or implementing that change effectively.

As Webb (2001) points out, organisations choose consultants for different reasons, for example political or ethical, where the advice given needs to be seen to be impartial; economic - using a consultant can be a very cost effective way of implementing change; or technical, where a particular expertise is required to resolve a particular problem.

Consultants can be used in many different types of project. For example:

- Auditing organisational information or knowledge resources.
- Reviewing the effectiveness of an information service.
- Carrying out a customer survey to assess the need for (or impact of) a new service or product.

- Preparing a user specification for the replacement of a library management system.

- Evaluating the effectiveness of an organisation's website.

- Researching the information needs of visually impaired library users.

There is clearly scope for a wide range of different behaviours depending on different circumstances: what Markham (1997) refers to as a continuum of consultancy behaviours. At one end is *client-centred* behaviour, where the consultant acts primarily as a facilitator, using the client's own experience and knowledge in an environment where the client wants some independence, wants to learn about and understand the problem, and make the key decisions. At the other end of the spectrum is the *consultant-centred* approach, where the consultant's specialised (and perhaps highly technical) knowledge is used to identify and evaluate options, formulate recommendations, and implement a solution in an area where the client has little or no expertise but recognises the problem is a pressing one. The important thing to remember is that both the problem and the solution need to be owned by the client: a consultancy project should always be a joint effort, and you will need to vary your role to get the best results.

Up to a few years ago, consultancy would end at the recommendation stage; increasingly, consultants are now expected to stay with assignments through the implementation process, and see the job through to the end. Whatever the role, the consultant will need influence if he or she is to create change. Influence is basically the exercise of power, and all consultants need to recognise that their power is their particular expertise, and that they should be confident about using it.

Personal qualities

The above implies a high degree of skill, and some essential personal qualities. Assuming that you already possess a degree of competence in your chosen area of operation, the following are vital to a successful consultancy career:

- a self-starter, able to work alone, and to keep motivating yourself when the going gets difficult

- strong analytical skills, and sound judgement

- good communication skills, both oral and written. You will need to be effective from the initial meeting with a prospective client, right through to the production of a final report, which may need to be delivered at a formal presentation

- excellent people skills: you may have to work with and gain the confidence of staff from clerical to board level

- a strong client focus, and the will to deliver a high value, professional service

- able to manage projects to time and budget

- flexible and adaptable - you will often have to juggle several things simultaneously, so an ability to prioritise is useful

- a belief in yourself: if you're hesitant about your own abilities, why should others be confident that you can deliver?

Cockman, Evans and Reynolds (1999) include a detailed consulting skills checklist to help you identify the skills required to become a successful, client-centred consultant. This is set out under headings such as 'Knowing myself', 'Communication skills', 'Observation and feedback skills' and 'Team building' and is a valuable tool for identifying areas of competence, and those that need development – or indeed those that you need to do less. It has been said that all consultants share the same feeling on Day 1 of a new assignment - apprehension and challenge. If that adrenalin buzz is alarming rather than stimulating, you're probably not going to be very happy as a consultant.

Can you afford it?

So, you have marketable experience, the right skills and qualities, and you're keen to get started. But before you jump, you need to ask yourself - can I afford it? Many people begin their consultancy career on the basis of a redundancy payment, or perhaps the promise of a substantial period of guaranteed work from a previous employer. For those without such a cushion, there are sums to do.

The following are just some of the possible costs involved in a start-up:

- Stationery: the cost will obviously vary, depending on whether you have a logo designed, full colour printing etc. and how many sheets/business cards you order. In these days of electronic communication, there is less need to stockpile boxes of expensive letter headed paper, but you will still need some, and business cards and compliments slips are essential. If your business will involve submitting multiple paper copies of tenders, or presenting formal reports to your clients, you may think that report covers, printed with the company name, are a good investment.

- Computer and other equipment: do you need a new PC, printer, modem, fax machine, answering machine, scanner, photocopier? How well does equipment that combines several of these functions actually perform? What is the cost per copy from printers and copiers? If you're home-based, will you require a new dedicated phone line, ISDN or ASDL?

- Office equipment and supplies: you can save money by going to a good second hand office equipment supplier for your filing cabinet, workstation and other office furniture. Try to keep office supplies down to what you really need: you can run up surprising amounts very quickly, once you start buying hanging files, folders and computer consumables.

- Premises, if you're renting space.

- Companies House registration costs of £20, if you're setting up a limited company in the UK, and an annual fee (currently £35) for registration under the Data Protection Act.

- Insurance: what you take out and how much it costs will obviously depend on personal circumstances, but you should certainly consider business insurance and Professional Indemnity Insurance (a prerequisite for some contracts). There are also various kinds of health insurance which you may need to consider in the event of being unable to work for a long time, or permanently.

- Professional fees: certainly an accountant; possibly also a solicitor.

- National Insurance Contributions and perhaps a personal pension, if hitherto you've had a company one.

- Business advice: very little of this is free.

- Advertising in the professional press.

You can, with very little effort, find that you've run up a four-figure sum even before you've received your first enquiry. If you have received your first enquiry, and it turns into a job, it may still be several months before you see any payment. Negotiating a contract can often take weeks from first meeting to a signed agreement. It is common to invoice monthly in arrears, and even more common for creditors to take at least 30 days to pay - many will try to get away with longer. If you have to wait months for your first payment, how well will you and any dependents cope? Even if work is coming in, you will have to learn to live with uncertainty, and the immutable law which lays down that you either have three jobs on the go or none at all.

One essential is to formulate a personal survival budget - to log, thoroughly and truthfully, everything you need to spend in order to live. This will include mortgage or rent, insurance of various kinds, pensions, household expenses, utilities, car, etc. and should also have a 'contingencies' heading for emergencies.

Working from home

There can be many advantages in working from home. Your overheads will be lower, you will not have to commute to an office, and a home office can be set up very easily. You may be able to manage your time much more flexibly. These obvious advantages can sometimes obscure the downside of home working, particularly if you have always gone out to work. However, you do need to consider the disadvantages as well, and be quite honest with yourself about how much weight they carry in your particular circumstances. For example:

- Isolation: how well do you work alone?

- Disruption to family life.

- You will need more discipline to put in a working day.

- It may be difficult to expand the business, or to bring other people in.

- It may be inappropriate to meet prospective clients or associates on home premises.

Very flexible arrangements are now offered for renting business units, and it may be worthwhile investigating what is available in your area.

If you do decide to work from home, you will be able to claim a certain amount against tax for heating, lighting and cleaning. However, beware of setting aside a specific part of your home as business premises, even if you're allowed to do so under tenancy or mortgage agreements. You could become liable for uniform business rate, and also for Capital Gains Tax on that part of your home when you come to sell it.

Legal Matters

How will you trade? If you are setting up in business in the UK there are three options:

Sole trader

As a sole trader, you are personally liable for the debts of your business. You will need to register as a self-employed person, and under Schedule D you will pay income tax twice a year, in January and July. You will also have to pay Class 2 National Insurance Contributions. It is probably a good idea at the start to set up a separate account for your income tax payments into which you can pay a percentage - say 20% - of your income.

Partnership

In a partnership, each partner is taxed on their share of the profits and are individually and collectively responsible for the total debts of the business. Partnerships can be tricky - you will need to get a formal partnership agreement drawn up by a solicitor, covering rights and obligations of the parties concerned.

Limited company

A limited company is a separate legal entity, so as a Director you are not personally liable for the debts of the business (unless you have pledged personal assets as security). You should check the current law on this as this could always change.You will have to lodge your Memorandum and articles of trading with Companies House and produce a set of audited accounts each year. You will also have to register your name before you start trading: sole traders and partnerships can start trading straightaway using their own names.

Whatever and wherever you are, you should consider putting together a statement of Terms and Conditions of trading, or a model contract for the supply of consultancy services, to give you a measure of legal protection. This might cover, for example:

- a statement of the services to be provided, that can be agreed by both sides

- a daily rate, and whether that includes VAT (value added tax)

- payment of other expenses, e.g. travel costs

- credit terms, e.g. 'payment due within 30 days of invoice date'

- definition of a 'day' in terms of working hours; will you charge for travel time?

- an undertaking to keep confidential all information connected with the client's business

- copyright statement for original material produced by you

- cancellation or termination of contract

- whether your company subscribes to any particular code of professional conduct.

It might be worth having two documents - one, a short one-page statement, which could go out to all clients, and a full, formal contract for weightier projects, which would require the signature of a senior manager in the client organisation. Either way, it is advisable to have professional advice on the wording of such documents.

Another legal issue to consider is that of Professional Indemnity. There is a debate within the consultancy profession as to whether this is useful or not. Partly it will depend on whether you are operating in client environments where this is insisted on - for example certain public sector bodies - but you may feel that it provides useful reassurance anyway, and underlines your professional standing. Typically, you will be asked to fill in a proposal form which gives details of your business, the qualifications and professional memberships of its principal officers, whether you use or intend to use subcontractors, estimated annual fee income and a breakdown for this in terms of geographical area (e.g. EU member states, USA and Canada) and activity (e.g. Strategic consultancy, Marketing, IT, Training, Project management), details of previous contract size. The company will then obtain a quote from their underwriters.

The insurance will cover legal liability to pay damages including all costs and expenses incurred in the investigation, defence or settlement or any claim arising out of negligent acts, errors or omissions. It may also cover libel and slander, loss of documents, dishonesty of employees, and unintentional breaches of copyright or confidentiality.

Moving on to money matters, a first priority will be to get yourself a good accountant - for 'good' read someone you can trust and work with and who, ideally, has had some experience of working with self-employed professionals rather than, for example, the manufacturing sector or fast food retailers, whose problems are likely to be rather different. An early decision which your accountant can help with will be whether or not to register for VAT or its equivalent. You will have to register in the UK if you expect your turnover to exceed £54,000 (2002 figure). This may sound ambitious for year 1, but will depend to a large extent on the kinds of contracts you expect to bid for, e.g. your target market may be contracts of £20k plus in which you plan to subcontract a percentage of the work, so £54,000 might be reached quite quickly.

There are other reasons for registering for VAT:

- if you do use subcontractors, you may well have to pay their VAT, and it is useful if you can claim this back

- if you expect to incur substantial business costs, e.g. for new computer equipment or office furniture

- it can help with cashflow: VAT is due quarterly, so VAT-inclusive payments received at the beginning of the quarter can be utilised

- don't ignore the PR aspect: a VAT registration number gives you an extra bit of credibility and weight.

Another early task will be to set up a business account - it is vital that from day 1 you can separate out your personal and business expenses. All the high street banks offer services to small businesses, and some have substantial information packs and videos to try to tempt new business. It is worth shopping around and comparing services and costs: many will offer 12 months free banking to start-ups, but existing account holders may be offered up to 2 years without charge. Beyond the 'free' period, transaction charges can be quite steep and do vary from bank to bank, so these should be checked out.

Your accountant can advise you on setting up a basic set of accounts. These need not be complicated, but they must be auditable, so form an early habit of never throwing receipts away, and noting down every payment!

Allied to a good set of accounts is a good filing system, so that you can track progress with prospects, clients and projects. It is worth taking time at the start to set up sound administrative and financial procedures. With any luck, you won't have time later on!

The Business Plan

You will have to have a Business Plan if you are trying to borrow money, but otherwise, is it worth it? Consultancy is all feast or famine - how can you possibly guess how much work you are going to get in? It is difficult, but look at it this way: if you don't know where you're going, you're never going to get there, and putting a plan together can be extremely valuable for clarifying thoughts and ideas. This should cover the following areas:

- Business objectives: what do you want to achieve in the long term, and what milestones will you set to get there? How realistic are they?

- If you're a partnership or limited company, what does your skills-set look like? What experience and knowledge of the industry do the principal players have?

- Will your location provide any particular competitive advantage?

- Equipment and its current value. When will you expect to replace? Do you foresee any capital expenditure costs over the next 12 months?

- What services or products do you offer, and what is unique about them?

- On what basis do you price your service, and how does that compare with your competitors?

- How many potential clients do you have? What are the strengths of your business that will persuade them to buy your services? Have you researched likely demand?

- Who are your major competitors, and what are their strengths and weaknesses?

- What level of sales do you anticipate over the next six months? What makes you think your forecasts are realistic?

- What are your start up costs and financial projections for gross profit, overheads, turnover?

Whether or not you put together a formal business plan, you will certainly need to put together a cashflow forecast, with predicted income levels and outgoings for things like salaries (e.g. yours!), insurance, postage, transport, telephone and telecommunications charges, professional fees and subscriptions.

Model business plans and cashflow outlines are readily available free from banks or business support agencies.

Marketing and Promotion

No matter how good you are, or how sought after your expertise, you will not get any business if nobody knows what you're offering and where to contact you.

A basic marketing plan is a good place to start. Which particular market sectors will you target? How many contacts do you have in your target sectors, and how will you reach them? Are there consultancies whose skills are complementary to yours which it would be useful to approach? Many consultancies, both large and small, have a pool of Associate Consultants who can be pulled in for relevant bids on an *ad hoc* basis. Over what timescale will your plan extend, and how will you judge its success or failure? Each of your target sectors will probably call for a different CV or résumé, highlighting a particular facet of your skills or experience. If you can, try to get these looked over by someone within the sector who can give you some constructive criticism.

You will need to try to identify sources of formal announcements of consultancy contracts: for example, newsgroups will provide occasional leads to consultancy work, the Resource website will include calls for tender, or you may pick up a published call for expressions of interest. There is an increasing number of websites listing details of consultants, but at the time of writing there are few that seem to be oriented towards consultancy in the LIS field. However it could be useful for you to register with one of these so that your name is in the public domain. Some offer free registration. Eventually, you can hope for follow-on work from existing clients or to get referrals through them. The sad fact is though, that when you're starting out you're not on anybody's list of consultancy companies to approach, and putting yourself in the way of opportunities at just the right time calls for a degree of luck. But you can help yourself by putting together a targeted marketing campaign, e.g. to organisations of a particular type or a particular sector, so that your interest and expertise is registered, and as your career expands you too can feature on the shortlists as being of known ability.

Whatever you do should be characterised by a professional approach. This covers business stationery, a 'house' style for letters and invoices, a consistent way of presenting proposals and reports - setting up a series of templates will save time, as well as looking businesslike. It goes without saying that your telephone manner will be courteous and professional - and that you will try to prevent your five year old, however engaging, from answering the telephone during office hours.

Advertising requires some thought, as well as possibly substantial amounts of money. Advertising rates for journals, and entry in yearbooks and directories, can vary and need to be costed out and the benefits assessed. How many potential clients are likely to see your ad? Is it worthwhile advertising somewhere on a regular basis, e.g. a particular professional journal? Do people notice, consciously or subliminally? If you miss an issue, will they think you've gone out of business?

Many consultancy firms have a brochure - they are handy for delegate packs, mailouts and inserts. People can pick them up and file them against some future need. They do require a lot of planning, though, since you need to make sure the message you are trying to get across is absolutely clear, and (depending on your type and length of project) they could have a limited shelf life. Where your specialism is fairly narrow, they can be extremely useful; less so if you are operating across a broad spectrum of activities, where a range of targeted 'profiles' may be more effective.

Increasingly, the expectation is that you as a consultant will have your own website, and there are some very good examples of sites put up by sole traders or small information consultancies. The best of these are where the consultant is well known in a particular sphere, and the site is not just an ad for their services but has information which is interesting in its own right - articles or bibliographies on the particular topic, or links to other websites. Again, the need is for planning, and you will have to take on board ongoing maintenance and updating. This may mean upgrading your own skills, so that you can do this yourself.

There are many other actions you can take to raise your profile – but note that these all take time!

- Get yourself onto any reviewing panel for professional publications such as *Managing Information* - editors are often delighted to hear from new reviewers - or offer to test information products for *Information World Review.*

- Write an article which demonstrates your expertise, perhaps based around a case study of a project (though be careful of client confidentiality).

- Persuade someone to profile you in a journal article or newsletter.

- Write or contribute to a book.

- Put yourself forward for election onto a professional committee.

- Take part in discussion lists, so that your name is associated with ideas and expertise in particular topic areas.

- Offer to speak at a conference, participate in a training event, or chair a session.

Whilst you are doing this on your own behalf, others can be marketing for you. Agencies are not just useful if you're job hunting - a few also handle consultancy assignments, or have consultancy operations themselves which use external Associates to supplement their own skills base.

But probably the most effective way of marketing yourself is networking and more networking. Attend professional meetings, talk to other consultants, in similar or complementary areas to your own. Keep in touch with them. Bear them in mind for joint bids, or joint promotional activities. You will sometimes be in competition, but there may well also be opportunities for collaboration. The world of the information professional is still quite small, and there is a lot of scope for mutual support and information swapping. There is no more enjoyable way of finding out what's going on!

Operating on your own can have problems and pitfalls. It can sometimes be lonely. It can also be immensely satisfying. If you enjoy challenge and variety, meeting different people and getting your teeth into substantial problems, there is nothing like it. By its nature, consultancy is an activity focused on change for the better - how many occupations offer a real opportunity to make a positive difference? Let us see what some of those currently working independently have to say about it.

Case study 5

After many years of working for the oil industry, Jean Etherton decided to broaden her horizons and go independent. Her decision coincided with that of her husband to sell his main electrical engineering business and run a secondary business from home. For both of them this constituted a mid-life change of work style. There were mutual benefits in that she was able to take advantage of his considerable business experience and acumen, whilst he gained valuable information input when she set up databases to assist his activities. There were further benefits in the sharing of office space and equipment. It is important in the running of any business that one has access to all the essential tools, so they ensured that computers, printers, fax, photocopier, and a range of software packages were all available.

Jean planned to offer those services of which she had most experience – the organisation and management of library and information services, desk and online research, and specialist knowledge of the energy industries. However, she recognised the need to remain flexible and found herself learning new skills and moving into new subject fields. Her main area of work today involves the setting up or reorganisation of library and information systems, which includes evaluation and survey as well as practical implementation of the systems. Her clients are drawn from a wide range of companies, professional and educational bodies, and local authorities - in the fields of law, insurance, marketing, social services, as well as the energy industries. She feels that one of the most interesting aspects of the job are the insights gained into the work of the different organisations that she visits. Since one can never guarantee an evenly spread work load, Jean found it useful to have a second string to her bow. Writing market research reports for a specialist publisher provides her with an activity during the less busy periods.

She was mindful of the fact that the hardest part of going it alone is finding work, after which actually doing the work may seem easy. The work itself always presents new challenges which can be daunting at the outset but invariably bring a sense of achievement on completion. To her, customer satisfaction makes it all seem worthwhile. She recalls one of her early clients who throughout the duration of a 3 month project, rather disconcertingly expressed no opinion on how the project was progressing until she presented the final bill. The client then declared 'we consider the money very well spent'. It was the best recommendation she could have asked for!

What qualities has Jean found essential to an information consultant? Undoubtedly, she says 'interpersonal skills coupled with professional ability, you need both of these – there are many people out there with the ability to do the job but far fewer who can communicate effectively with the client, and then there are those with the persuasive skills but without the professional expertise to do the job. The client will soon realise if the consultant is ineffective and will not offer repeat work.'

The marketing process of competing with other consultants and preparation of proposals were all new activities for Jean and something that she had to learn from scratch, but she feels that she has now honed these skills to a high level. 'Sometimes the reasons for losing a job to a competitor are beyond one's control - it may be because your competitor has specialist experience in a particular field, or there can be in-house political reasons for awarding contracts to one consultant over another.'

What has she gained from the experience? Jean says that she learned to identify and develop her particular strengths – organisational skills and people management coupled with a very personal service offered. She uses temporary staff to work with her on projects, some of whom are her regular employees of proven track record. They tend to do the more routine tasks of sorting, classifying, and inputting to computer systems. Most clients are only too pleased to have someone who is able to manage and organise a project for them, leaving them to get on with their main operation.

And her final comments 'Being independent is not for the faint hearted, there are plenty of disappointments - contracts won but then not carried out because the client has changed its mind or been taken over. However when things go well it can be exciting, challenging and fulfilling'.

Case study 6

Bob Bater had already spent 11 years in his first career as an industrial chemist, when he encountered 'information' as a discrete, and challenging concept. 'Almost overnight, I learned that the effective management of intangible concepts such as 'information' underpinned everything I had been doing to manipulate the interaction of diverse molecules in crafted conditions for defined commercial ends. It was a true revelation. Although it was not an easy decision, with a wife and 10-year old child to consider, I was 'hooked' on this thing called 'information' and decided to leave the chemical industry and attend library school to learn more about it. I went to 'CLW' (the College of Librarianship Wales) in Aberystwyth as a mature student when it was still an independent college, and almost overnight, life seemed to undergo a complete transformation.'

On leaving library school, Bob spent some time as a freelance researcher for a London-based publisher, and then got a full-time job as a special librarian in an engineering consultancy, where 'I first encountered IT and realized that it was a vital ally to my chosen profession.' A period of exploration of the ways in which IT could support the use of information led to a post as New Technology Manager within the National Health Service (NHS). It was to prove his route into consultancy. 'That post provided me with invaluable experience in IT, IT management, business planning and management, and team management, but in addition it offered an opportunity to continue my exploration of the potential for synergy between IT and information use. Ironically, it was the NHS reforms of the 1990 Thatcher government that were to provide the opportunity for me to become independent. When my employing organization was restructured and a voluntary redundancy package became available, I opted for a redundancy offer which involved no payment but re-engaged me and my team of four as contractors, to provide much the same portfolio of services as before.'

He gives two reasons for eschewing the possibility of a moderate redundancy windfall in favour of a more risky option: 'Firstly, my Myers-Briggs personality profile (INFP, for those who might be interested), identifies me firmly as a 'crusader', so it was no surprise to find myself wanting to turn the tables on the *status quo* and start promoting the benefits of applying information science principles to IT systems. The advent of the Internet only served to reinforce my conviction that information was the focal concept and that technology was vital but secondary. On the one hand, there was the information profession, struggling on without the undeniable benefits offered by IT; and on the other, there were the Web techies, designing search engines in blissful unawareness of 130 years of information science. There was a lot of work to be done to bring the two camps together in a common purpose, and I wanted to make a start on it.

My second reason for going solo stemmed, I think, from my brief time as a freelance researcher after leaving library school. I had enjoyed being a 'free spirit' and escaping the constraints of employment, which determined both the location in which I needed to reside, the hours I worked, and most importantly, the scope of application of my competences. I wanted time to explore what I could do, to set and follow my own agenda, and to have control of my own future.'

Increasingly, Bob found himself developing what he saw as a key element of information management – the need to align information resources and technology with business objectives. This proved to be a real uphill struggle. 'For some reason, the idea of 'information management' had failed to register with the organisational elite, and it was to be the knowledge management (KM) phenomenon which opened corporate eyes to the value of the hybrid mix of business, information science and IT skills I possessed. When KM came along, I finally recognized a context in which my vision became meaningful to organisational decision-makers. It provided the opportunity I had long sought to make a final leap out of the IT box and into KM.'

As Bob sees it, the very core of information work has always been the ability to mediate between available information resources and the idiosyncratic needs of individual users and groups. This applies equally at the user-PC interface as at the enquiry desk. Consultants and advisors to organisations on information and knowledge management today need to understand the dynamics of person-to-person and group interaction, as well as the characteristics of information resources and the technology which can support their exploitation. The value contributed by knowledge and information is moderated by the context of its use - individuals and their working environment, including working conditions, peer and manager relationships, and an often uneasy tension between personal ambition and corporate goals.

'I find that professional updating is a cornerstone of my own consultancy practice and certainly takes up a lot of my time. Because I work primarily at the interface between information resources and IT, I need to be aware of current practice in both fields. And because people are the key actors at that interface, I like to maintain a 'toolkit' of techniques and technologies which are designed to interact with people, rather than network servers. Obviously, the core set of information science techniques are in there – classification, indexing, taxonomy, thesauri – as well as the most relevant IT-related ones – database technology, intranets and HTML, digital resource metadata and now, of course, RDF (Resource Description Framework), XML (Extensible Markup Language) and topic maps. But so also are interviewing skills, knowledge elicitation techniques and presentation skills. Where a job might require skills I don't have, I make sure I keep in contact with other freelance colleagues who do. I have undertaken a number of projects on that sort of collaborative basis.'

Like many consultants, Bob regards the greatest danger for the lone consultant as isolation. 'I can update my professional knowledge nowadays through membership of various online mailing lists & newsletters and online forums, but I make sure I maintain membership of two or three professional networks for that face-to-face contact for which there is no substitute. I am a member of the former Institute of Information Scientists (now merged with the Library Association to form CILIP) and Aslib and of the Aslib IRM (Information Resources Management) Network, and the latter, in particular, has proved invaluable in helping me to feel I am a member of a community. I am also an associate of a fairly new network called IncoNet (independent consultants' network) which draws together independent practitioners right across the spectrum, not just KM. The next greatest danger comes from the blurred distinction between work and the rest of life. If you have a partner and/or close family, they need to be very supportive and understanding. It is just so easy to yield to the pressures and let work squeeze everything else out. We've all been there at one time or another, I'm sure.'

For Bob, networking doesn't simply combat isolation, but is the major channel through which business opportunities arise. Advertising has never worked for him, though he acknowledges that relying on word of mouth can be risky: 'there can be long gaps between commissions, which in turn can lead to alarming fluctuations in cashflow. Building up some kind of cash reserve to see you through the dips is vital, although the non-fee-earning time isn't wasted – you can use it to update yourself, learn new things, and generally grow the business. As you become established, you can make yourself less sensitive to these dips in income, because you learn how to push your day rate up to what the market can stand. But that can take some considerable time, and you'll need to draw on all your reserves, and not just financial ones. You need motivation, commitment and stamina and to take the constant uncertainty in your stride.' Would he go back to being employed? 'Well, apart from the fact that employment is no longer the safe haven it was – no way!'

Case study 7

Monitan Information Consultants was established in 1982 as a solo consultancy by Monica Anderton. At the time, it was set up as a limited company. Like Bob Bater, Monica is a career scientist by training. Following an Honours degree at Sheffield University and a Masters in Animal Science at the University of Nottingham School of Agriculture, her first job was as a scientific officer, working for the Ministry of Agriculture, Fisheries and Food in their Central Veterinary Laboratories in Weybridge. This was pure science, in a team environment. As a result of some collaborative work with Vickers Medical Research (as it was then), she was headhunted to another scientific position, this time in industry, moving to Newcastle in the process. The work was based on early developments in the biotechnology industry, which was then in its infancy. Initially, she worked as a practising scientist, but as time went by, she gradually got more and more involved in the informational aspects of the work, doing market and technical research for the parent group of companies. That was in the days when the only people allowed to do on-line searches were the mathematicians in the computing department!

By the early 1980s, for various political reasons, the Biotechnology division was closed and the personnel went their own ways: in Monica's case, to providing an information service in the life science sector, specialising in Biotechnology, based on market and technical research with the added value of subject knowledge. She comments 'in some ways it was easier to set up as a solo consultant than to find work elsewhere, as the majority of relevant positions would be based in London and the South East and the North is very good to live in. Unfortunately, the locational limitation is still true today, despite the setting up of a new biotechnology initiative in the region, which is the third in the last 20 years.' Monica has been trying to sell the benefits of quality information to business for 20 years and finds it is as difficult now as it was originally.

There was little external help for entrepreneurs in those days and financing was difficult. With hindsight, Monica believes that setting up a limited liability company was not necessarily the best way to proceed and indeed, Monitan was delisted some 6/7 years ago. Going from corporate person to sole practitioner did not cause many problems. Monica seemed to have a knack for the business side, and is these days closely involved with the small and micro-business sector – 'the backbone of British industry and service'. She often gives talks on the subject to both students and to other practitioners, new or otherwise. 'Consultants always want to know how every one else is doing their business.'

Monica never wished to grow a large business, and is happy as a sole operator, networking and collaborating with other professional colleagues when the need arises. The networking aspects of life are very important to her, as is keeping up both with the technical aspects of work and the practical aspects of business: copyright, data protection, employment law (usually relating to clients) and so on. 'The meetings and courses and network provided by one's professional bodies is invaluable and the old boy/girl network is a wonderful Mafia.'

Monica points out that changes in government support of industry and business have caused problems to Monitan and other consultants in the region and elsewhere. Whilst early schemes were attractive and provided work for consultants and benefits to clients, the later schemes which became heavily subsidised started undercutting the work done by Monica and her colleagues. 'Low cost or free services are difficult to compete against and to the client, free is generally perceived as better, even if the quality of advice was often inferior. One can join up and work from the inside, but again the terms and conditions are not always desirable to any one with high professional standards.'

She finds that the main problem in working as an individual is in getting support when things do go wrong, which fortunately is not often. But it does occur and taking advice from experts does help to mitigate problems. She quotes an example of helping out a colleague who was owed a considerable sum of money and who was not getting paid, in spite of having done the work well, because the prime client refused to pay. This is the harder sort of lesson to learn and she believes it happens to more consultants than are prepared to admit it.

Motivation has never been a problem; working from home as Monica now does keeps the overheads down nicely and doesn't present too many obstacles. 'One of the major problems is that one is always there, 24 hours a day and some people think you'll answer the phone accordingly.' Having spent many years with an office in the next door county, Monica also maintains a PO Box. This keeps her in touch with the local business sector.

She reflects 'Over the years one's motivations do change; from wanting to be a hugely successful business person to the more realistic aim of enjoying one's work and providing a valuable service. If this means less work but better jobs, that's OK. Evening out the cash flow can be a trial as a sole trader but being one's own boss is better than working for someone else, excluding the client!'

Case study 8

Monica Blake has worked as an independent information consultant since 1981. It was redundancy that provided the impetus to go it alone: as a translator for the database publisher Information Retrieval Limited (IRL), she was one of 40 people laid off when the company sold its database to Cambridge Scientific Abstracts. At the time, she was halfway through a part-time postgraduate course in information science, and freelance work offered the opportunity of completing this course.

Beginning with translation and editorial projects for publishers, she moved on to research work. During the mid-1980s she carried out a number of projects for the Primary Communications Research Centre at the University of Leicester. After this centre closed down, the main funding bodies for her research became the British Library Research & Development Department (and its successors) and the BNB Research Fund. Her research interests range from information and society to scholarly communication. She has conducted several projects on teleworking and has written widely on the subject. Other research studies have included journal cancellations in university libraries, electronic archiving, academics' use of foreign language material, and the Internet and older people. She has retained an interest in editing: from 1983 to 1986 she edited *Inform*, the newsletter of the Institute of Information Scientists, and from 1993 to 2001 was Editor of *Online and CD Notes*.

One of the major challenges of working as an independent consultant is keeping abreast of change, particularly technical change. This involves not only budgeting for expenditure on ICT but also allowing time to learn how to use it effectively. Monica began with a borrowed manual typewriter, and moved on through an electric typewriter and an Amstrad to various generations of PCs. Along the way, she has learned to use different software packages and has acquired Web skills.

Finding time to keep up to date in the field is a concern of many LIS professionals. Working independently involves being especially proactive about getting access to resources. Monica's strategies include belonging to professional bodies for their journals and newsletters, visiting libraries with good LIS collections, attending conferences, and using the Internet. She has found professional bodies to be helpful, not only as sources of information, but also in providing opportunities for networking. Serving on the committees of such organisations has led to the formation of both friendships and professional contacts.

Monica has written elsewhere about the drawbacks and benefits of working independently (e.g. *Teleworking for Library and Information Professionals*, Aslib, 1999). In her own experience, she has found the greatest difficulty to be coping with major life changes such as moving house: while an employee can take time off when needed, this is much harder for an independent worker. On the plus side, she values the rich diversity of work available to an information consultant. Although research and editing have continued to be central to her work, Monica has enjoyed a variety of one-off assignments. Some have involved her knowledge of German: for example, in 1990, when CD-ROM was in its infancy, she travelled to Germany to demonstrate databases using this technology in university libraries. Other work has included a review of open plan working for the British Library when it was planning staff working space for the move to the new building at St Pancras, teaching at the then University of North London, and writing for various publications.

Case study 9

Leonard Will took a first degree in physics and went on to do research in that area. The need to collect and organise bibliographic references for his research, and his marriage to a librarian, led to his developing an interest in scientific information work. The satisfaction of being able to solve other people's problems by finding information effectively in the literature proved more rewarding than research in a fairly obscure area of physics, and he took the opportunity to move to a post in charge of information and research services in a university library. Computerised information systems were at that time in their infancy, and offered exciting areas for development.

Some years later he moved to the Science Museum, with the role of computerising the library there and advising on the computerisation of the records of museum objects. This new post combined information work with a broad area of science and technology, and provided an opportunity to enter at ground level on the newly developing area of museum documentation. He rose to become Head of Library and Information Services, and as the library had substantial collections of pictorial and archival material he was able to become familiar with the techniques of these specialities. With seniority, however, his work became more administrative and he had fewer opportunities to tackle the technical problems that he enjoyed. In 1993 the Museum decided that it had to cut staff in order to save money, and invited applications for early retirement. Leonard applied and left the Museum in January 1994 at the age of 52.

As early retirement provided a modest pension income, he was not under urgent pressure to earn money, but wanted to continue to develop his professional skills and to do interesting work. Consultancy seemed an excellent way to achieve this, and he decided to call himself an 'information management consultant', thus covering information work in museums, libraries and archives, which were just beginning to recognise that they shared many problems. The mechanics of setting up in business were fairly straightforward, the investigation of requirements regarding tax, accountancy, insurance, forms of contract and so on being just another application of information retrieval skills. He decided to do his own accounting, but used a lawyer on the Internet to draw up a general-purpose form of contract for consultancy work.

As he had been actively involved in various professional bodies, he had quite a range of contacts and was sufficiently well-known so that finding work was never a problem. There were certainly gaps, which would have been worrying if this was a sole source of income, but he had as much work as he wanted. He considers that it is important to keep a sufficiently high profile, by attending meetings, contributing to e-mail discussion lists and newsgroups, and by developing a website which not only advertised his availability for consultancy work but also provided useful information that encouraged people to visit it. The main features of this kind were an introductory paper on the principles of building and using an information retrieval thesaurus and a directory of software packages for thesaurus development and management. Maintaining this, keeping up to date in the broad field he covers, some voluntary work (e.g. maintaining Web pages for two of his professional bodies) and administration of the business amply fill any gaps between paid contracts.

His wife, Sheena, meantime, had pursued her library career, working in public, academic and government libraries and finally in the British Library where she first did bibliographic and subject indexing work and then on-line searching for the public in the patents information service. In 1996 she left the library and joined Leonard in his consultancy work; they established a partnership with the title "Willpower Information" – a pun on their name, which has proved to be usefully memorable.

The kinds of work done are very varied, which adds to the attraction of the job. While a specialisation in subject indexing and thesaurus work has been developed, Willpower Information is prepared to tackle any project which they feel competent to do well and which provides sufficient interest and challenge. Projects completed include drawing up technical specifications for the procurement of library and museum software, surveying the status of archives in all UK universities, assessing bids for funds for a grant-giving organisation, converting museum databases from Microsoft Access into a major, Oracle-based collections management system, teaching the documentation module of a master's degree course in Amsterdam, running a week-long documentation course in Egypt, and working on thesaurus development on topics as diverse as place-names, ethnography, musical instruments, natural history, fossils and maritime objects.

They measure the success of the business as much by the interest and satisfaction that it brings as by the income earned. Although it now brings in enough to live on, a lot of stress is removed by having a pension income buffer. Nevertheless the work is much more than a sideline – it has to be run professionally and the confidence of clients has to be maintained. No deadlines have ever been missed, even though it may mean many long days to achieve this, and clients are not invoiced until they have had a chance to say that they are satisfied with the products. Overheads are small, the main expenses being attendance at professional conferences and meetings at home and abroad – luckily these are tax-deductible! Adequate computer hardware and software is essential, and the Internet is the main means of communication with clients and colleagues as well as a major source of information in the absence of an institutional library.

The Internet too provides the continuous contact that would otherwise be missing for someone working from home, not only on professional matters but also including the chat and gossip that allows a consultant to keep in touch with developments, trends and attitudes. Leonard and Sheena have no wish to develop the business to the extent of employing staff, as one of the main attractions is the lack of responsibility for managing other people. Although they have worked jointly with other consultants on some projects, the need to coordinate work and the fact that they do not have complete control over the finished product generally make this a less attractive option. They are happy to take personal responsibility for the work that they deliver.

Final advice

David Haynes, who ran his own very successful consultancy company for many years before joining CILIP as its first Head of Consultancy Services in 2002, has some sound advice for anyone thinking of information consultancy: "This is an exciting and demanding career choice. However do not launch yourself into self-employment without first securing work to take you through the initial months of the new business. Too many people have given up their jobs on the basis of a vague promise 'get in touch when you have left, I may well have some work for you'. You need to be confident about your abilities and resilient. You need optimism to consider that every opportunity will turn into work and the resilience to pick yourself up off the floor when an opportunity does not bear fruit". His last piece of advice is "be visible – go to professional meetings, attend conferences and seminars, even better get to speak, write articles, send out press releases celebrating your successes or reporting your findings (if you are doing research). Consultancy is an exciting career but one that is particularly subject to change – expect the basis of your work and the market that you operate in to be different in 5 years time."

The examples given serve to illustrate the wide potential for personal development as an independent consultant. Though they have different histories and different backgrounds, all our cases demonstrate the need for energy, enthusiasm and good organisational and communication skills, backed up by excellent and up-to-date professional and subject knowledge.

Printed References

Cockman, Peter, Evans, Bill and Reynolds, Peter (1999)
Consulting for real people: a client-centred approach for change agents and leaders. 2nd edn. London: McGraw Hill

Markham, Calvert (1997)
Practical management consultancy. 3rd edn. Milton Keynes: Accountancy Books

Webb, Sylvia P. (2001)
'The independent consultant', *Information Management Report* May, pp. 1-5

Web site References

Resource: the Council for Museums, Archives and Libraries www.resource.gov.uk/

Chapter 8

Continuing to develop

Throughout the previous chapters we have looked at a range of possible development opportunities. Examples have been provided of people who have sought and achieved personal development within their work environment, combining learning with improving the service which they offer. This can occur within a single organisation, or in several, as in the case of the independent consultant. What about professional development that does not directly result from the individual's day-to-day work? How and where does that take place? It certainly does not come about just by chance, you have to seek it out and work at it.

First you will need to assess what stage you have already reached. How far along the path of personal development have you ventured, and where should you go from here? You could go back to the first chapter and revisit the two exercises there, adding new activities and areas of responsibility, and analysing your responses to them. That would certainly be a useful starting point in terms of identifying what further opportunities there may be in your current job, or in a new role either with your current employing organisation or elsewhere.

A useful new tool which could help you to assess and review your skills capability, and to decide on a possible future career direction, is the skills toolkit developed by TFPL specifically for those working in the fields of Information or Knowledge Management. Its aim is to help individuals compare their own skills against certain identified benchmarks. These come in the form of various skills profiles which relate to different roles in terms of scope and seniority.

The toolkit allows individuals to identify gaps in their existing skills make-up and to seek ways of filling these, or of strengthening and updating skills which they already have in place. It provides a means of assessing the skills needed for any current role, and of considering those which an individual might want to acquire for future career moves. The toolkit also provides some useful links to development resources which could help in the process. TFPL's Skills Toolkit was launched in April 2003 following extensive pilot testing, in both the public and private sectors. The pilot tests identified a number of potential uses by individuals and management: for example it could help individuals to measure their own skills against the mix of skills and levels required by current and future roles; enable managers to assess the skills requirement of various roles or tasks, and provide a means of assessing the level and type of skill held by individuals and within teams. The skills are graphically presented using spidergrams which can be overlaid to illustrate skills gaps. Skills profiles for sample roles are provided. The toolkit also points to ways of developing skills, reflecting different learning styles and resources. The toolkit is available to individuals via the TFPL web site and can be purchased for wider internal use in organisations. More information can be found on the web site (*www.tfpl.com*). This suggests one way of re-assessing your career potential and setting in train your own development programme. Other ways of assessing management capabilities and potential are also suggested in chapters 1, 3 & 7.

Today, change takes place quickly and has a global impact, whether in terms of economic, technological or social change. There is a strong need for **research** across the whole area of library and information service policy and activity, given broader organisational developments which affect those services. Research aims to identify areas for change, and ways of achieving this; aiding decision making and setting standards. Those working in LIS will have as second nature the ability to seek data and trace sources, but carrying out a research project requires much more. First identifying an area which requires research; secondly putting together a proposal aimed at obtaining funding to support it; and thirdly having the necessary skills to conduct the research. For example, in the field of business research, you will not only need an understanding of the area of business under consideration and knowledge of relevant information sources, but also the analytical skills and ability to use related methodologies to produce results. Webb, T (1998) discusses the importance of monitoring research activity to encompass both the conduct of the research and the use made of its outputs. He identifies key principles which should be incorporated into the research process, whatever the size of the business and wherever the research activity is located in the organisation. He also notes the importance of maintaining consistency of quality throughout.

Any research proposal must be clear and well-structured, setting out the reasons for the research, its aims, methodology, and hoped-for outcomes. This must be accompanied by a clear statement and breakdown of costs and timing, so those general management skills that you have acquired will come into their own for this process.

Various bodies can be approached for research funding. Some grants may be provided jointly by more than one organisation. Keep an eye on the general press as well as on publications in the LIS and academic fields, for example the *Times Higher Education Supplement*, where calls for proposals and invitations to tender may appear. Start making a list of bodies which operate grants schemes, such as the Nuffield Foundation Social Science Small Grants Scheme, which is a rolling programme, or JISC (Joint Information Systems Committee) which has regularly funded research into the Managed Learning Environment. Resource: the Council for Museums, Archives and Libraries, commissions research in the domains within its remit. At the time of writing they are seeking to support projects which look at collaboration between libraries and education, especially cross-sectoral arrangements. Monitor the websites of such organisations so that you do not miss any opportunities. Apart from the subject matter of research there is tremendous personal development to be achieved in designing and conducting a research study. However small it may be, it requires analytical and communication skills as well as the ability to manage projects and to design and use appropriate research tools and methods.

LIS managers in all sectors are increasingly needing to **evaluate the service** that they provide, in some cases to provide evidence in support of changes they wish to make, or additional resources which they require; or even to justify their continued existence. This is no longer likely to be able to be carried out just by a simple survey. You may also have to set your services and procedures against benchmarks and performance measures, so you will certainly have to be up-to-date with what is going on in those areas. For a practical guide to evaluating your service, see Crawford (2000). You may also want to incorporate performance measures into any assessment and evaluation programme. A report which looked at performance indicators in public libraries and school libraries was the result of work carried out by Information Management Associates (2000) for the former Libraries and Information Commission, now Resource. The project generated a substantial number of guidance materials for libraries; these are now available on the *www.informat.org* site. Thornton and Stewart (2001) of the Defence Science and Technology Laboratory (Dstl) a new agency of the UK's Ministry of Defence, provide an interesting approach to performance measurement. Not only is Dstl a new agency, but the unit in which Thornton and Stewart have their responsibilities, is also a new department, namely Knowledge Services. They argue that the traditional notion of the service level agreement does not go far enough, usually consisting solely of the performance measurement of operations. They suggest that this should be taken further and additionally measure business support performance. They describe their progress so far in developing a framework for the creation of a useful and more meaningful service level agreement for Dstl Knowledge Services. For some further thoughts on performance measurement you might also have a look at Parker and Crawford (2001).

The **information audit** has long been seen as a useful tool for assessing and evaluating LIS, in order to make changes in response to expressed needs. It also acts as a cornerstone on which to build an information strategy as Thornton (2001) suggests in his review of audit methods and possible successful outcomes. He sees the information audit as providing an important link between the business strategy and the information policy of an organisation; essential to be viewed in tandem for optimum effectiveness. So the information audit and the pursuit of an information strategy/policy provide further fields for self-development. You will find some good examples of information policies in Orna (1999), which will also give you a lot of useful ideas about how to present your case.

As noted in chapter 2, **benchmarking** is now taking place in a number of libraries, and tools have been developed to assist with this. The original concept was designed to allow measurement of the whole organisation against others; seeking to establish best practice as a benchmark. Some of the earlier discussion relating to such developments in LIS can be found in an issue of the journal *Special Libraries*, Summer, 1993 which was devoted to the subjects of benchmarking, total quality management & the learning organisation. [This journal is now entitled *Information Outlook*]. Since then benchmarks have gradually been developed to allow specific departments like LIS to measure their performance against others either inside or outside their own organisation and sector. A particularly useful manual has been produced by SCONUL (2001), which although initially based on experiences in the academic sector, is in looseleaf form so that LIS from all sectors can add their own material on processes and procedures specific to them.

Managing change is itself an area which offers considerable scope for personal development as well as research, as demonstrated very ably by Gallacher (1999) who emphasises the range of skills needed to achieve change in LIS, and suggests a number of mechanisms available in the general management field to help in this. Pugh (2000) also provides a thorough introduction to the subject of change and considers related problems with solutions applicable to LIS in the academic, public and commercial sectors.

Change affects all types of organisation and all functions within it, including the LIS. The following examples of change show that skills that perhaps you have not had to develop earlier, may now be called for. These two examples have been provided by Kathy Roddy, an independent fundraising and management consultant who has worked in libraries in the public, academic and voluntary sectors. Contact details are given in the Appendix.

Example: Fundraising skills

"The funding climate for libraries in most sectors – the public, academic and voluntary sectors in particular - is changing rapidly and there is now a greater expectation for libraries to generate a proportion of their funding from external sources. This may be for special projects or for day-to-day running costs. Indeed, many academic libraries and a small number of public services have sought and obtained charitable status in order to take advantage of tax-efficient fundraising methods and gain access to grantmaking trusts and foundations which support academic, literary and community activities.

Librarians will, in most cases, be well equipped in terms of skills to undertake the research necessary to identify potential funders and to establish appropriate systems for managing the processes involved in making applications and acknowledging donors. However, fundraising is a highly complex and greatly misunderstood activity and its success depends upon having the appropriate infrastructure and evaluation systems in place. It is by no means a simple matter of finding a potential donor and "asking for money".

Long-term planning, including financial planning, is crucial to the success of any fundraising campaign and the librarian or information manager intending to go down this road will certainly need to acquire new knowledge with respect to the kind of organisational and legal structures necessary to obtain charitable status, fundraising legislation and the financial reporting requirements which charities are expected to meet."

As the above example demonstrates, the ability to derive a persuasive case for support from the library's long-term planning document and to construct a fundraising strategy will also require an understanding of fundraising methods and the context within which fundraising takes place. So the whole gamut of management skills discussed in earlier chapters will be vital, especially the ability to make a business case and communicate it persuasively, based on a clear understanding of the legal and other implications.

Example: Managing volunteers

"Whilst the rate of change with respect to UK and European employment law makes it difficult to keep up-to-date, the trend of using volunteers within libraries* raises its own issues. LIS managers need to be aware that managing volunteers is a specific activity which, whilst it may have elements in common with managing other staff, has some very significant differences and contains certain pitfalls of which you need to be aware.

The decision to use volunteers can be a real opportunity for libraries and information centres to develop their services and help others into the profession. However, volunteers are not "cheap labour" and should never be regarded as such. Any decision to provide payment to volunteers, however minimal, may potentially be seen as conferring employment rights. The same applies where volunteers are expected to make a regular time commitment. Mistakes in these areas can be very expensive for employers – some volunteers have taken the organisations they have been working for to UK Employment Tribunals and have won. Such outcomes then have further consequences in terms of tax and national insurance**. Employers may also fall foul of the UK's Minimum Wage requirements or similar legislation in other jurisdictions.

As with fundraising, the decision to use volunteers within the LIS must be a strategic one with clear policies and procedures in place for managing the process. Involving staff in this process is crucial to ensure that the decision to use volunteers is not seen as an underhand way to replace staff or something which could downgrade the profession. Any member of staff who is expected to manage volunteers should have this in their job description in recognition of the importance of the function and time must be allowed for staff members to undergo the necessary training in volunteer management.

*A study reported in the February 2001 issue of the *Library Association Record* (now replaced by CILIP's *Update*) showed that 85 public library services in England made use of volunteers. Across the UK as a whole, the figure averaged 61%. However, only 39% of London Boroughs used volunteers.

**Migrant Advisory Service v Chaudri (18.09.98 EAT/1400/97) and Armitage v Relate (8 December 1994; Case No 43538/94)"

Both Kathy Roddy's examples indicate that if you take on such responsibilities, which may be new to your organisation as well as to you, the importance of finding out what is involved and developing new skills accordingly is of the utmost importance. This is where professional contacts and networking can really come into their own; where you can learn from the experience of others what may be needed and what the possible pitfalls and benefits might be. As with other trends, these could also prove to be useful areas to explore further via research.

Whichever direction you choose, you need to consider where your skills would be most useful, and what you may need to add, especially if you plan to change sectors. Recent research into the skills requirements of senior information managers in the Higher Education (HE) sector provides some interesting insights into this. The Higher Education Funding Council for England (HEFCE), through its Fund for Good Management Practice, awarded funding to the University of Birmingham to carry out a project into succession planning for senior staff in information services in the HE sector. The Centre for Information Research (CIRT) at the University of Central England was commissioned to undertake the research phase of the project known as **HIMSS (Hybrid Information Management: Skills for Senior Staff)**, having a proven track record in the library, information and education fields, especially in delivering research with transferable outcomes that feed into practice. The following detailed discussion of the project has been included with the kind permission of both institutions.

In particular, the HIMSS project was to explore whether problems with recruitment at this level existed and, if so, whether such problems were caused by aspiring heads of services not possessing skills required for heads of services posts. Library, computing and converged information services (either academic and administrative computing services or computing and library services) were all included in the scope of the project.

Data was collected through surveys with four different groups: aspiring heads of information services, newly appointed heads of information services, senior managers with direct line management responsibility for heads of information services, and directors of personnel.

The research concluded that the roles of heads of information services were becoming more hybrid, and generic management skills and personal qualities were overwhelmingly identified as the most important attributes for a head of information services. Well-developed generic management skills were considered particularly important for heads of converged information services managing cross-functional teams.

Training & development activities recommended to overcome the apparent lack of such skills included: formal courses, mentoring, shadowing, secondments, professional networks, peer group support networks, profession-wide seminars, conferences and meetings, and regular job reviews including personal development plans.

The research recommends that information services staff aspiring to higher positions should:

- make time for self-development
- ensure that self-development is undertaken within an appropriate framework, recognising that high-level posts require more generic management skills
- take advantage of performance appraisals, training opportunities, secondments, networking etc, treating these as part of their career development
- be prepared to move around (within and outside the sector) to gain the necessary experience
- plan their career paths before they reach the level of a deputy.

It is also suggested that employers should provide appropriate management experience for early aspirants to senior management posts, including fast tracking, local succession planning opportunities and training provision.

According to some of the participants the HE sector was seen as operating like a 'closed market' in respect of appointments to senior posts in information services. It was regarded by many, especially in IT, as a less attractive option than other sectors. So if you are considering changing sectors make sure you know not only what is needed but also what the culture is likely to accept.

The HIMSS study also noted that some specialist skills and knowledge were identified as important for success as a head of information services in certain posts. The need for specialist skills along with general management skills is well-illustrated in another piece of work carried out by CIRT, described in an article by Thebridge & Matthews (2000). In this they set out under a number of headings the range of activities and necessary skills and knowledge required for the various elements of preservation management. This article could act as a useful model for those drawing up job specifications in other fields. Contact details for CIRT are listed in the Appendix.

The field of **preservation management** has been receiving renewed attention, particularly in relation to digital material. Schlicke (2002) raises the key issues and arguments in her discussion of current and recent projects in this area. She notes the potential benefits to users, librarians and publishers, seeing digital preservation as a vital part of collection management and acquisitions policy. This whole area could present the LIS manager with considerable scope for personal development, as well as for developing the service.

As you build up your own skills and ways of handling situations, others may also be able to benefit from your experiences. Now is the time to start ploughing back that knowledge into **the wider profession**. This can happen in a number of ways, through involvement in the professional associations; participation in the activities of formal and informal groups; membership of working parties and committees, often set up with a specific brief to look at certain issues; contributing to external training; lecturing; writing. Most professional associations have regional branches, providing a point of reference and activity for members who may be spread geographically. In Australia and the USA, where distances between centres are so much greater than in the UK, state groups fulfil this role.

These all provide means of sharing ideas with other members of the profession and, by doing so, sharpening your own awareness of professional matters and heightening your personal level of motivation and career satisfaction. This can also bring about positive spin-off for other staff in your department, as well as influencing the operation of certain tasks.

The professional associations provide a point of reference for everyone who carries out library and information work, regardless of the type of work environment, or level at which you operate. That point of reference is always there, but the more you use it, the more useful you will find it becomes. An association can only be as good as its members, therefore high-quality input by members results in high-quality output to members. So have a look at what is currently going on; see how you can not only make the most of what they have to offer, but also contribute.

What do such associations offer their members, both in terms of direct services, and opportunities for participation through which personal development will come about? It is not intended to list here every activity of each association - for that you should consult the web site or literature produced by the individual bodies. The intention is rather to indicate the scope for individual involvement.

The formal structures of the associations are described in their various constitutions. Policies are usually made by an association's council, with related discussion and work being carried out by various committees whose remits will range from education and employment to information technology. As a council or committee member you would stand to learn a lot, as well as to contribute.

The activities of the associations extend far beyond their own manifest purpose, not just looking after members' interests in any narrow sense, but campaigning on wider issues which may influence members in their working practices and long-term planning. In doing so they represent a collective voice to government and other official bodies, not just on matters of professional concern but also on those of wider cultural significance, e.g. copyright, freedom of information.

Education and training are major concerns of professional bodies, as is lobbying and advising other authorities which have responsibility for providing or supporting the range of LIS which fall within the information services sector. They can offer careers advice and recruitment opportunities. Most also have significant publishing interests, organise conferences, run courses, and above all provide the opportunity to network with other members of the profession. This may be face-to-face through special interest groups, at meetings, or via a discussion forum on the Web. So the focus of your personal development might be in such activities.

It is important to view your own service in **the wider context**, not only by sector, but also by country. A good way to start if you are working in the UK or any other European country is to look at *www.eblida.org* the website of EBLIDA, the European Bureau of Library, Information and Documentation Associations. This is an independent umbrella association of national institutions in Europe, which concentrates on information society issues ranging from copyright to culture and education. EBLIDA publishes news in hard copy for its members as well as offering it more widely one month later on the website, where it also lists its latest and recent projects, press releases and a host of other interesting items of information, which could well trigger ideas for you to pursue.

Organisations offering vocational qualifications not only in LIS-related fields, but in many other business and professional areas e.g. management, law, finance, could also make use of your skills. There are significant developments arising from closer links with professional education and training agencies throughout the rest of the world. Look at websites of the British Council *www.britishcouncil.org* and other bodies with an international remit for some indication of this.

Such outside involvement is essential to all those who wish to remain professionally alert, but is of particular value to the lone operator. Even if it is difficult to get to meetings during the working day, many group activities take place in the evening. Where there is resistance from an employing organisation to daytime attendance, you should perhaps put into practice the use of some of those persuasive skills discussed in earlier chapters, pointing out the direct benefits to the organisation of your attendance, e.g. good public relations, making new contacts, as well as the possibility of getting new ideas for the service. Make a point of taking along any new publicity material produced by your organisation which could be of interest to some of the participants. Actively look through any attendance lists which may be sent in advance of a meeting. Go prepared with questions to which you need answers, problems which need solving - someone there might be able to help.

In addition to the professional associations and their various interest groups and branches, there are a number of other formal and informal groups in which you might become active. These tend to focus on LIS within particular sectors such as law, health, finance, and others, and provide considerable opportunity for networking and learning. They can also be demanding as they rely on the enthusiastic and committed participation of their members often in their own time. But this is more than repaid by the personal development that individuals experience through such involvement. These groups may have a web site, publish journals or newsletters and arrange visits, workshops and conferences which are usually lively and interesting events. (See Appendix.)

From the breadth of activity described, you will see the scope for personal development within the work of professional associations and related LIS-focussed bodies. In addition to the associations set up specifically with the LIS profession in mind, there are others which can contribute considerably to personal development. Those are the organisations which are concerned with the improvement of various aspects of working life, e.g. management activities and training, human resources, commercial and legal matters, all of which are highly relevant to the management role of the librarian or information worker. Some of these have already been mentioned elsewhere and are listed in the Appendix. There are many others which could be relevant depending on your particular interest, work role and the sector in which you work. So have a look through any listing of associations, for example, those published by CBD Research, which cover a number of different countries and sectors and are available in print or electronic form. You may be surprised at how many of those associations listed could be useful.

Copyright and freedom of information are mentioned above as being subject areas in which LIS professional associations are naturally interested. However these are of just as much interest to the LIS manager, not least because he or she may well be the person controlling access to, or reproduction of information in the work place. These and related areas which have legal implications such as intellectual property and data protection offer considerable scope for further learning. The regular use of electronic sources, and the ease with which data can be transmitted, make it particularly important for LIS staff to be fully conversant with the law which aims to protect such information and its owners. This is thoroughly discussed by Marrett (2000) in the second edition of his book *Information law in practice.*

Some time ago Webb (1997) questioned whether there was still a role for the information professional, noting that most other professions were expected to have information skills in addition to their other qualifications. The question is still being asked but the answer could at least in part lie in the CIRT research mentioned earlier. To be a successful information manager you are likely to need to have not only information skills and subject knowledge, but also the ability to perform a range of management functions, maintaining flexibility and being alert to change.

The development of such competencies should not be viewed by the individual as ceasing on the completion of formal studies. In fact it is at this point that development really begins, and continues throughout the individual's career. A survey undertaken jointly by the Association of Graduate Recruiters (AGR) and the *Financial Times,* found that career success for graduates depended less on their qualifications than on their eagerness to learn new skills. The AGR has as its members many of the UK's top employers, who were asked to rank various factors as indicators of a graduate's likely long-term success. A propensity for further training scored very highly, with readiness to learn seen as a top priority in the workplace. The results of the survey are described in the *Financial Times, 11/12 May 2002, Top Universities Suppl. p.1,* and contact details for the AGR are given in the Appendix.

Sheila Corrall, Director of Academic Support Services at the University of Southampton, in her recent conference paper, Corrall (2002), considers the future roles of information professionals. She looks in particular at the skills and attributes that will be required for effective performance and the commitment needed to develop a learning workforce. Corrall notes two areas demanding special attention: 1) our evolving role as information educators, and 2) the current shortage of professional leaders. Both these areas would seem to offer considerable scope for personal development.

As the information professional starts to put his or her skills into practice - making decisions, solving problems, seeking new approaches and techniques - development will take place and prove to be of benefit to both the individual and the employing organisation. There are numerous opportunities out there, but the onus is on you to identify and make the most of them - it is well worth the effort.

References

Association of Graduate Recruiters/*Financial Times* (2002)
Financial Times, 11/12 May, Top Universities Suppl. p.1

"Benchmarking, total quality management & the learning organisation: new paradigms for the information environment" (Summer, 1993)
A collection of articles in a special issue of the journal *Special Libraries*. Washington: Special Libraries Association [N.B. This journal has now been re-named *Information Outlook*]

Corrall, Sheila (2002)
Skills for the future. A paper presented to the LAI/CILIP NI annual conference, Belfast, April 2002

Crawford, John (2000)
Evaluation of library and information services. 2nd edition.
London: Aslib.

Dalton, Pete and Nankivell, Clare (2002)
HIMSS. Hybrid Information Management: Skills for Senior Staff. Final research report and recommendations. Birmingham: CIRT [At the time of writing this is available in electronic form only from:
www.himss.bham.ac.uk/Final%Research%20Report.pdf]

Gallacher, Cathryn (1999)
Managing change in libraries and information services. London: Aslib

Information Management Associates (2000)
Best value and better performance in libraries. Library and Information Commission Research Report 52. London: Library & Information Commission

Marrett, Paul (2002)
Information law in practice. 2nd edition. Aldershot: Ashgate

Orna, Elizabeth (1999)
Practical information policies. 2nd edition. Aldershot: Gower

Parker, Sandra and Crawford, Marshall (2001)
Performance measurement and metrics. Chapter 6 in Scammell, A., ed. *Handbook of Information Management*. 8th edition. London: Aslib

Pugh, Lyndon (2000)
Change management in information services. Aldershot: Ashgate

SCONUL (2001)
SCONUL Benchmarking manual edited by J. Stephen Town. London: SCONUL

Schlicke, Priscilla (2002)
Born - and re-born -digital
Information Management Report, July, pp. 1-4

Thebridge, Stella and Matthews, Graham (2000)
Skills and knowledge required for preservation management.
Personnel, Training and Education, December 2000, pp.6-9

Thornton, Steve (2001)
Information audits. Chapter 5 in Scammell, A., ed. *Handbook of Information Management.* 8th edition, London: Aslib

Thornton, Steve and Stewart, Chrissie (2001)
A new look at service level agreements. 4th Northumbria International Conference on performance measures in libraries and information services: "Meaningful measures for emerging realities". Pittsburgh, PA, 12-16 August 2001, pp.263-266

Webb, Sylvia P. (1997)
Thoroughbred or hybrid - the information manager in the 1990s?
Information Management Report, October, pp. 1-4

Webb, Trevor J. (1998)
Researching for business: avoiding the "nice to know" trap. London : Aslib

Appendix: Useful addresses

Key organisations

Book Aid International
2 Coldharbour Place
39-41 Coldharbour Lane
Camberwell
London
SE5 9NR
Tel: +44 (0)20 7733 3577
Fax: +44 (0)20 7978 8006
e-mail: info@bookaid.org
www.bookaid.org/

British Council Information Centre
Bridgewater House
58 Whitworth Street
Manchester M1 6BB
Tel: +44 (0)161 957 7755
Fax: +44 (0)161 957 7762
e-mail: general.enquiries@britishcouncil.org
www.britishcouncil.org

Chartered Institute of Library and Information Professionals (CILIP)
7 Ridgmount Street
London
WC1E 7AE
Tel: +44 (0)20 7255 0500
Fax: +44 (0)20 7255 0501
e-mail: info@cilip.org.uk
www.cilip.org.uk/

Chartered Institute of Personnel and Development
CIPD House
Camp Road
London
SW19 4UX
Tel: +44 (0)20 8971 9000
Fax: +44 (0)20 8263 3333
e-mail: various, according to nature of enquiry
www.cipd.co.uk/

Companies House (London office):
PO Box 29019
21 Bloomsbury Street
London
WC1B 3XD
Tel: +44 (0)870 3333636
Fax: +44 (0)29 20380900
e-mail facility on web site
www.companies-house.gov.uk/

European Bureau of Library, Information and Documentation Associations (EBLIDA)
Teresa Hackett, Director
PO Box 43300
NL-2504 AH
The Hague
The Netherlands
Tel: +31 70 309 0608
Fax: +31 70 309 0708
e-mail: eblida@nblc.nl
www.eblida.org

Office of the Information Commissioner
Wycliffe House
Water Lane
Wilmslow
Cheshire
SK9 5AF
Tel: +44 (0)1625 545740
Fax: +44 (0)1625 524510
e-mail (General enquiries): data@dataprotection.gov.uk
www.dataprotection.gov.uk/

Society of Archivists
Hon. Sec. Mark Weaver
AstraZeneca R & D
Charwood
Bakewell Road
Loughborough
Leics. LE11 5RH
Tel: +44 (0)1509 644195
Fax: +44 (0)1509 645570
e-mail: mark,weaver@astrazeneca.com
www.archives.org.uk

Society of College, National and University Libraries
(SCONUL)
102 Euston Street
London
NW1 2HA
Tel: +44 (0)20 7387 0317
Fax: +44 (0)20 7303 3197
e-mail: sconul@sconul.ac.uk
www.sconul.ac.uk

Organisations offering training and advice

Association of Graduate Recruiters
Innovation Centre
Warwick Technology Park
Gallows Hill
Warwick CV34 6UW
Tel: +44 (0)1926 623236
Fax: +44 (0)1926 623237
www.agr.org.uk

Capita Learning and Development
(previously Industrial Society Learning and Development)
17 Rochester Row
London
SW1P 1LA
Tel: +44 (0)870 400 1000
e-mail: info@capita-ld.co.uk
www.capita-ld.co.uk

Chartered Management Institute
Management House
Cottingham Road
Corby
Northants
NN17 1TT
Tel: +44 (0)1536 204222
Fax: +44 (0)1536 201651
www.managers.org.uk

Cimtech Limited
University of Hertfordshire
45 Grosvenor Road
St Albans
AL1 3AW
Tel: +44 (0)1727 813651
Fax: +44 (0)1727 813649
e-mail: c.cimtech@herts.ac.uk
www.cimtech.co.uk/

City & Guilds of London Institute
1 Giltspur Street
London EC1A 9DD
Tel: +44 (0)20 7294 2468
Fax: +44 (0)20 7294 2400
e-mail: enquiry@city-and-guilds.co.uk
www.city-and-guilds.co.uk/

City University
Department of Information Science
Northampton Square
London
EC1V 0HB
Tel: +44 (0)20 7477 8381
Fax: +44 (0)20 7040 5070
e-mail (Continuing Education): conted@city.ac.uk
www.city.ac.uk/

Edinburgh's Telford College
Crewe Toll
Edinburgh
EH4 2NZ
Tel: +44 (0)131 332 2491
Fax: +44 (0)131 343 1218
e-mail: mail@ed-coll.ac.uk
www.ed-coll.ac.uk/

Industrial Society Learning & Development
(see Capita Learning and Development)

London Metropolitan University
Applied Social Sciences
Ladbroke House
62-66 Highbury Grove
London
N5 2AD
Tel (Course enquiries): +44 (0)20 7753 3355 (Undergraduates); +44 (0) 20 7753 3333 (Postgraduates)
e-mail: admissions.north@londonmet.ac.uk
www.londonmet.ac.uk

TFPL Training
17-18 Britton Street
London
EC1M 5TL
Tel: +44 (0)20 7251 5522
Fax: +44 (0)20 7251 8318
e-mail: training@tfpl.com
www.tfpl.com/

University College of Wales, Aberystwyth
Department of Information Studies
Llanbadarn Fawr
Aberystwyth
Ceredigion
SY23 3AS
Tel: +44 (0)1970 622182
e-mail: jye@aber.ac.uk
www.dil.aber.ac.uk/

Video Arts Group
Dumbarton House
68 Oxford Street
London
WID 1LH
Tel: +44 (0)20 7637 7288
e-mail: enquiries@videoarts.co.uk
www.videoarts.com

Recruitment agencies

Aslib Professional Recruitment Ltd
Temple Avenue
3-7 Temple Chambers
London EC4Y 0HP
Tel: +44 (0)20 7583 8900
Fax: +44 (0)20 7583 8401
e-mail: recruit@aslib.com
www.aslib.co.uk/recruit/

Glen Recruitment
18 Southampton Place
Holborn
London
WC1A 2AX
Tel: +44 (0)20 7745 7245
Fax: +44 (0)20 7745 7244
e-mail: info@glenrecruitment.co.uk
www.glenrecruitment.co.uk/

InfoMatch
Chartered Institute of Library and Information Professionals
7 Ridgmount Street
London
WC1E 7AE
Tel: +44 (0)20 7255 0570
Fax: +44 (0)20 7255 0571
e-mail: infomatch@cilip.org.uk
www.cilip.org.uk/employ/infomatch.html

Instant Library Recruitment
104b St John Street
London
EC1M 4EH
Tel: +44 (0)20 7608 1414
Fax: +44 (0)20 7608 1038
e-mail: recruitment@instant-library.com
www.instant-library.com/

Personnel Resources
75 Grays Inn Road
London
WC1X 8US
Tel: +44 (0)20 7242 6321
Fax: +44 (0)20 7831 7121
e-mail: jobs@personnelresources.co.uk
www.personnelresources.co.uk/

Phee Farrer Jones
1st Floor
10 Alfred Place
London
WC1E 7EE
Tel: +44 (0)20 7854 8800
Fax: +44 (0)20 7854 8885
e-mail: enquiries@pfj.co.uk
www.pheefarrerjones.co.uk/

Price Jamieson
Pricejamieson House
104-108 Oxford Street
London
W1D 1LP
Tel: +44 (0)20 7580 7702
Fax: +44 (0)20 7436 4789
e-mail: recruit@pricejam.com
www.pricejam.com/

Recruit Media Ltd
20 Colebrooke Row
London
N1 8AP
Tel: +44 (0)20 7704 1227
Fax: +44 (0)20 7704 1370
e-mail: bizinfo@recruitmedia.co.uk
www.recruitmedia.co.uk/

Sue Hill Recruitment and Services Ltd
Borough House
80 Borough High Street
London
SE1 1LL
Tel: +44 (0)20 7378 7068
Fax: +44 (0)20 7378 6838
e-mail: jobs@suehill.com
www.suehill.com/

TFPL Recruitment
17-18 Britton Street
London
EC1M 5TL
Tel: +44 (0)20 7251 5522
Fax: +44 (0)20 7251 8318
e-mail: recruitment@tfpl.com
www.tfpl.com/

Consultancy and research

Information Services
University of Birmingham
Edgbaston
Birmingham
B15 2TT
Tel: +44 (0)121 414 5817
e-mail: library@bham.ac.uk
www.is.bham.ac.uk

Kathy Roddy Research and Consultancy
11 Queenswood Gardens
Wanstead
London
E11 3SE
Tel/Fax: +44 (0)20-8530-2843
e-mail: kathy@kroddy.fsnet.co.uk

Centre for Information Research (CIRT)
Faculty of Computing, Information and English
University of Central England
Dawson Building
Perry Barr
Birmingham B42 2SU
Tel: +44 (0) 121 331 5619
Fax: +44 (0) 121 331 5675
e-mail: cirt@uce.ac.uk

Research funding

Higher Education Funding Council England (HEFCE)
Northavon House
Coldharbour Lane
Bristol BS 16 1QD
Tel: +44 (0)117 931 7317
www.hefce.ac.uk

Joint Information Systems Committee (JISC)
Northavon House
Coldharbour Lane
Bristol
BS16 1QD
Tel: +44 (0)117 931 7385
Fax: +44 (0)117 931 7255
www.jisc.ac.uk

Resource
16 Queen Anne's Gate
London SW1H 9AA
Tel: +44 (0)20 7273 1452
www.resource.gov.uk

Nuffield Foundation
28 Bedford Square
London WC1B 3JS
tel: +44 (0)20 7580 7434 (24 hour answerphone - ask for Small Grants applications materials)
www.nuffieldfoundation.org

Sources of library statistics mentioned in the text

Library and Information Statistics Unit (LISU)
Loughborough University
Loughborough
Leics. LE11 3TU
Tel: +44 (0)1509 223070
Fax: +44 (0)1509 223072
www.lboro.ac.uk/departments/dis/lisu

Swets Blackwell
Swan House
Wyndyke Furlong
Abingdon Business Park
Abingdon
Oxfordshire OX14 1UQ
Tel: +44 (0)1235 857500
Fax: +44 (0)1235 857501
www.swetsblackwell.com

Consultants featuring in Chapter 7

Monica Anderton
Sandyford
Healey
Riding Mill
Northumberland
NE44 6BA
Tel: +44 (0)1434 682496

Bob Bater
InfoPlex Associates
43 Ashley Down Road
Horsfield
Bristol
BS7 9JN
Tel: +44 (0)1179 441368
e-mail: infoplex@online.rednet.co.uk

Monica Blake
114 Glenarm Road
London
E5 0NA
Tel: +44 (0)20 8986 7828
e-mail: mblake@cix.compulink.co.uk

Jean Etherton
Jean Etherton and Associates
Summerhill
3 Little Common
Stanmore
Middlesex
HA7 3BZ
Tel: +44 (0)20 8954 7302
e-mail: jeanetherton@sml.co.uk

Leonard Will
Willpower Information
27 Calshot Way
Enfield
Middlesex
EN2 7BQ
Tel: +44 (0)20 8372 0092
e-mail: L.Will@Willpowerinfo.co.uk
www.willpowerinfo.co.uk/

Special Interest Groups

For details of the branches and groups of the professional associations, contact the individual associations.

There are also a number of independent groups. As these are largely informal groupings the contact details frequently change. They are therefore not listed here, but it is relatively simple to trace them by approaching the LIS manager in one of the major firms or organisations working in your field; e.g. law, health, accountancy, insurance. A listing was produced in Webb, Sylvia P(1996) *Creating an Information service* 3rd edition, London: Aslib, pp.115-116, which will give you some idea of the range of groups available at that time, and although the contact details are likely to have changed, the person listed could probably point you in the right direction.

Index

Italic letters after page numbers indicate these types of content:
a = address
b = bibliographic reference
c = case study
w = website reference

transferable skills 30
Travica, Robert 93
ttsp 86

U
University College of Wales, Department of Information Studies 29, 95, 139*a*
University of Birmingham 126, 142*a*
University of Central England, Centre for Information Research 126, 128, 143*a*
University of London, Central Information Service 4
University of North London 95
user interviews 23, 46

V
VAT (value-added tax) registration 105
Video Arts Group 51, 58, 74-5, 79*b*, 139*a*
video-recording, in training 58
Viles, Ann 93, 97*b*
virtual reference interviews 93
volunteers, management of 125-6

W
Webb, Sylvia P 8, 10, 11*b*, 15, 19, 20, 37, 66, 82, 84, 99, 119*b*, 131, 133*b*, 145*b*
Webb, Trevor 122, 133*b*
Westminster City Libraries 37
Will, Leonard (Willpower Information) 116-18*c*, 145*a*
Withers, Bill 75, 79*b*
word processing software 69
work placement 29-30
Work Placement 29, 44*w*
working day, itemisation 5-7
working environment 14-17
World of Learning, The 38, 43*b*
writing, effective 72

Y
Yate, Martin J 46, 58*b*

$30.62 \times 1 = 30.62$

(no disc.)